SIR FRANCIS DRAKE

Behind the Pirate's Mask

ANDREW NORMAN

HALSGROVE

First published in Great Britain in 2004

Front cover and Frontispiece picture: *Portrait of Sir Francis Drake, by an unknown artist of the English School.*
Photo: By kind permission of H.M.S. *Drake*, HM Naval Base, Devonport, Plymouth.

British Library Cataloguing-in-Publication Data
A CIP record for this title is available from the British Library

ISBN 1 84114 371 5

HALSGROVE

Halsgrove House
Lower Moor Way
Tiverton, Devon EX16 6SS
Tel: 01884 243242
Fax: 01884 243325
email: sales@halsgrove.com
website: www.halsgrove.com

Printed and bound by
The Cromwell Press, Trowbridge

Contents

About the Author

Andrew Norman was born in Newbury, Berkshire, England in 1943. In 1956 his family moved to Southern Rhodesia (now Zimbabwe) and so witnessed the closing years of the colonial era. In 1959 the family returned to England, and in 1962 he went up to Oxford University, to St Edmund Hall. Having graduated in physiology he became a medical student at The Radcliffe Infirmary; qualifying as a doctor in 1970. He married in 1967 and has a son and daughter. In 1972 he went into general practice in Poole, Dorset. A serious back injury in 1983 forced his early retirement, and he is now a writer.

His other books include:-

HMS Hood: *Pride of he Royal Navy* – Stackpole Books, Mechanicsburg, P.A. U.S.A. (2001) – ISBN 0-8117-0789-X.

By Swords Divided: Corfe Castle in the Civil War – Halsgrove, Tiverton, U.K. (2003) – ISBN 1-84114-228-X.

Robert Mugabe and the Betrayal of Zimbabwe – McFarland & Company, Inc. Publishers, Jefferson, North Carolina, U.S.A. (2004)
– ISBN 0-7864-1686-6.

T.E. Lawrence: Unravelling the Enigma – Halsgrove, Tiverton, U.K. (2003)
– ISBN 1-84114-321-9.

Tyneham: the Lost Village of Dorset – Halsgrove, Tiverton, U.K. (2003) –
ISBN 1-84114-322-7.

Thomas Hardy: Behind the Inscrutable Smile – Halsgrove, Tiverton, U.K. (2004) – ISBN 1-84114-324-3.

Preface

To know Sir Francis Drake is to know adventure: to tramp with him through the jungles of Mexico in search of the Spanish 'treasure train'; to scour the seas for treasure ships; to set out to circumnavigate the globe in an age when many still believed the earth to be flat, and if one went too far one was likely to fall off the edge (where exactly on the east coast of North America Drake landed on his circumnavigation has long been a subject of lively debate, and remains so even today!); to make a pre-emptive strike on Cadiz (the so-called 'singeing of the King of Spain's beard'); to bring to battle the mighty Spanish Armada, where Drake was so confident of victory that he insisted on finishing his game of bowls before setting sail! But to know Drake is also to know extreme hardship: from the time when as a boy, he and his family were driven out of their home by Catholic rioters; to when he was shot in the face by a native Indian in South America, and in the leg by a Spanish musketeer in Mexico, and lost two brothers in his Spanish campaigns.

Yet beneath all this is a very different story, that of the REAL Sir Francis Drake, which can only be discovered by 'walking the walk', as it were. In other words, to visit Tavistock and the River Tavy where he fished as a boy; Plymouth, with its famous 'Hoe' anchorage, and 'Black Book' where passage of the Armada ships offshore in 1588 was recorded by the town clerk, who was an eye witness to the event; Sampford Spiney manor house where he is reputed to have spent his honeymoon; Buckland Abbey his home where many artefacts are kept including his famous drum; the tortuous roadway to Lopwell Quay, from which he would have caught the ferry-boat down river to Plymouth to where the great ships, his included, were anchored; the dwelling of his first wife Mary, humble in comparison to the huge stately pile of his second, the aristocratic Elizabeth.

The greatest insight, however, comes from reading his letters and the contemporary accounts of his relations, of historians, and of Englishman and Spaniards – both friends and foes alike!

᭡

My own interest in Drake arose when I discovered that I might be descended, in part at any rate, from the 'other side' as it were; for an ancestor of mine from Plymouth shares the same name (John – or Juan – Jago) as a survivor from the Armada hospital ship, the *San Pedro Mayor*, which was wrecked at Hope, near Salcombe. Could there be a connection, I wondered? Was it possible that Jago, and perhaps others taken prisoner from the ship, instead of returning to Spain on their release, remained in Drake's own county?

Such was the obscurity into which Drake was born that neither the year of his birth, nor the name of his mother is known for certain; and yet he rose to become vice admiral of the English Navy, and to all intents and purposes its leader in battle; and through his exploits, a legend even in his own lifetime. However, the purpose of this in-depth analysis is to discover the real Sir Francis Drake; to find out precisely what lies 'Behind the Pirate's Mask'.

Acknowledgements

I am indebted to Cdr C.W. Crichton OBE; The University of Exeter Press; City of Plymouth Museums and Art Gallery; The National Trust; Curator, Berkeley Castle; Palace of Westminster; Graham Kirkpatrick, Steward, Tavistock Museum; John and Rosalind Spedding.

Also to Rachel Dragffy, Jean Norman, Thomas Norman, Jane Savery, Keith Jarvis (Archaeological Officer, Waterfront Museum, Poole, Dorset), Jane Francis, Peter Devlin, Brian Speight and Tom Gillibrand.

The wind commands me away. Our ship is under sail. God grant we may so live in His fear, as the enemy may have cause to say that God doth fight for her Majesty as well abroad as at home, and give her long and happy life and ever victory against God's enemies and her Majesty's.

Sir Francis Drake
(before the attack on Cadiz).

1

Lowly Beginnings, but Powerful Connections

In the County of Devonshire, the name 'Drake' is first mentioned in the reign of King Henry III (1216-1272), when Reginald le Drake, and Ralf and Roger le Drake owned lands in Tiverton and Dartington, respectively.

The Drakes were one of several Devonshire seafaring families which included the Raleighs, Grenvilles and Gilberts. However, although Francis Drake was the person who, more than any other, saved England in 1588 from the Spanish Armada, it is an irony that so little is known of some of the pertinent details of his background, such as the date and year of his birth (and those of his siblings), the first name of his mother, and the date of her marriage to his father, Edmund. These records have not survived.

It is known that Francis Drake's grandparents were John Drake and his wife, Margery. They lived at Crowndale, a village a mile to the south-west of Tavistock on the River Tavy, on the western edge of Dartmoor, in the County of Devonshire. With the increase of tin mining in Devon, Tavistock became one of three 'stannary' (mining) towns to which the blocks of tin were brought, to be weighed, have a small corner chiselled off by the assay master, and then be stamped with the royal coat of arms. After this they could be sold.

The 'Drakes of Crowndale' were yeoman farmers, who for generations had rented 180 acres of land from the Benedictine Abbey of St Mary and St Rumon at Tavistock. In 1534, King Henry VIII renounced papal supremacy and proclaimed himself head of the English Church. As a consequence of this, two years later in 1536, during his Reformation, the smaller monasteries were dissolved by Act of Parliament, and the larger ones encouraged to surrender themselves to his authority.

When on March 3, 1539 the Royal Commissioner arrived in the town, John Peryn, the thirty-ninth abbot, summoned his twenty monks to surrender the monastery and everything belonging to it (including manors, churches, lands, buildings, books and parchments), into the

Tavistock Abbey: remains of Abbot's lodgings and Western Gatehouse.

hands of the King. The rich shrine of St Rumon was dismantled and its gold, silver and jewels conveyed to the Tower of London.

The fittings and furnishings were sold off cheaply; the lead was stripped from the church roof, and two pence was paid for 'the carryinge oute of (head) stones and bones oute of the churchyarde'. The Abbot was given a generous pension of £100 per annum for himself: his monks received pensions of between £2 and £10. [1]

In 1539, the year of the dissolution of Tavistock Abbey, there was controversy when the new 'Great Bible' was made compulsory reading in churches. This Bible, which had been translated into English from the Latin by Miles Coverdale (born 1488), was now accessible to anyone with the ability to read.

After the Dissolution, the Government set up a Council of the West with jurisdiction over Devon, Cornwall, Dorset and Somerset. The Dorset squire, John Russell, later to become Earl of Bedford, was appointed President of the Council, and was granted the site of the abbey and most of its former lands and possessions. He would now become the Drake family's new landlord.

These events caused mixed feelings amongst the local population. The monks were unpopular in that they levied a tithe of ten per cent of everything grown or manufactured, even the feathers from the breasts of fowls which had been killed and plucked! However, their charitable work in education and the relief of distress was sadly missed; although their hospital for lepers did continue to function for a time.

John and Margery Drake had six children (possibly seven), the second son of whom was Francis's father, Edmund, who is believed to have begun life as a sailor, and to have been an early convert to the Protestant faith. It is said that Edmund's travels to the ports of northern Europe led to his conversion to Protestantism.

The date of Edmund Drake's marriage (in about the year 1541) is not recorded, neither is the first name of his wife. However, it is believed that she was the daughter of a Richard Mylwaye, whose family lived in the parish of Upchurch, on the southern shores of Kent's River Medway, and near Gillingham Reach, home port of the Tudor navy. How then did the two meet, when the distance from Plymouth to Upchurch is 250 miles by land and even further by sea? Is it possible that Edmund had met his wife-to-be in his seafaring days on a chance visit to Kent? This must remain a matter for conjecture.

Edmund and his wife had twelve children, Francis, their eldest son being born in the year 1542 or 1543, presumably at Crowndale Farm. The custom in those days was for a person from the upper echelons of society to offer to be god-parent to a newly born child of his acquaintance. This being the case, Francis Russell (son of Lord John, the 1st Earl of Bedford, warden of the stannaries (tin mining districts) and Lord Lieutenant of Devon and Cornwall) became Drake's godfather (the child being named after him), and attended his christening. Although then only seventeen or eighteen years of age, Francis Russell was already a Member of Parliament and, like all the Russells, was in sympathy with the Protestant Reformation. By 1544, Edmund had returned from sea to Crowndale Farm.

In 1548 (the second year of the reign of King Edward VI, who was then only eleven years old) Plymouth's 'Black Book' (containing the names of its mayors and town ledger) refers to 'the Fyrst inssurreccyon in Cornwall', when the Catholic peasantry rioted in protest at the destruction of their sacred images. The riots were cruelly put down by Lord John Russell, and the leaders hanged, drawn and quartered. These included an unnamed 'traytor of Cornwall' on Plymouth Hoe. The authorities paid John Mathewe one shilling 'for carying a quarter of the traytor to Tavystoke' as a warning to the inhabitants; the young Francis Drake may well have gone down to the town with his family to witness this gruesome spectacle.

On Whit Sunday, 1549, Catholic peasantry throughout the land rose up to oppose the compulsory reading of the new (English) Book of Common Prayer, and to demand the enforcement of the Six Articles Act, which had been passed by King Henry VIII a decade previously. This Act affirmed the Real Presence (of the body and blood of Christ in the eucharist); that communion... is not necessary to salvation; that it was not permissable for priests to marry; that monastic vows were of perpetual obligation; that private masses ought to be continued; and that auricular confession ought to be maintained. According to the Black Book, there was a 'greatte insurrecccyon throughowte all the Royaulme (Realm) of Englonde (England), and esspecyally in the Counties of Deuon and Cornwalle'. The 'rebels' also demanded the restoration and re-endowment of the two chief monasteries in each county, which in the case of Devon would include Tavistock, with half of all seized abbey lands.

The revolt in the south-west started near Bodmin in Cornwall, from where Cornish Catholic rebels then crossed the River Tamar into Devon. The Black Book records that during this five-week period, 'the cytie of Excestre (Exeter) & the Castell of Plymmothe (Plymouth) were valyently defended & kepte from the Rebelles'. However, much damage appears to have been done, including the burning of Plymouth's 'stepell (tower)', and 'alle the townes evydence (documents)'.

As Edmund Drake's great grandson would later state, it was because of persecution (presumably by Catholics during the insurrection), that Edmund Drake was 'forced to fly from his house... into Kent (where his wife's family lived)... there to inhabit the hull of a ship, wherein many of his younger sons were born'.[2] He had twelve children in all.

Retribution followed, with 'the comyng of the lord Russell, lord privie seale & lord lieutenant (Drake's godfather)...', who, with his 'greate armye... subdued the said Rebells, of which were slayne at the same tyme a greate nombre, and diu'se (divers) put to execucyon owte of hand, and certayne taken pison (prisoner) & caryed to london and afterward hanged at Tyborne (Tyburn)'. With the crushing defeat of the rebels at Clyst St Mary, near Exeter, peace was restored to the county.

In 1553, Edmund Drake is recorded as being the curate at Upchurch, a region of increasing importance, it having now been declared that all royal ships should be 'herborowed' (harboured) in the Medway, including those hitherto at Portsmouth. Until then, Edmund had been employed as prayer-reader to the 'Fleet-Royall'.[3] So how did he obtain this position? After all, he was not a university graduate (though he knew sufficient Latin to be able to keep the church's records), and was therefore not permitted to preach. Instead he would normally have been expected to hire a licensed preacher four times a year to preach sermons for him. However, he was too poor to afford the fees.[4]

It is possible that John Russell secured this post for Edmund, who may also have been encouraged in his chosen career by his uncle, the priest William Drake. Uncle William Hawkins, the Plymouth shipping magnate, may also have played a part, as may Edmund's one time colleague, William Master, who was himself a priest.

Unfortunately for Edmund Drake, 1553 was the year that Edward VI died and the Catholic Mary Tudor (nicknamed 'Bloody Mary' for her savage persecution of Protestants), commenced her reign. The law against priestly marriage was now rigorously enforced, and this may have been what cost Edmund his job.

How Edmund occupied himself over the next six years is not known (he appears to have kept a low profile and may have returned to sea for a while), but in 1559, the year after Mary Tudor had been succeeded by the Protestant Queen Elizabeth, he was reappointed curate of Upchurch; John Townley being its vicar. Edmund's star was now in the ascendant, for on January 25, 1561, this 'clerk in holy orders' was instituted by Matthew Parker, Queen Elizabeth's first Archbishop of Canterbury, as 'vicar perpetual to the Parish of Upchurch in the diocese of Canterbury'. Edmund is now listed as an 'unmarried priest'. Had his wife died, or did he give himself this title purely as a matter of expediency?

As for Edmund's sons, including Francis, it is recorded that '... it pleased God to give most of them (the sons) a being (livelihood) upon the water'. Sadly, however, 'the greater part of them (the sons) died at sea'. Fortunately for England, as it transpired, Francis Drake was not one of their number!'[5]

In his will, made on December 26, 1566, shortly before his death, Edmund revealed his piety by advising his youngest son, Thomas, to 'make much of the Bible, that I do here send thee with the rest of the godly books'.

Although Francis Drake had no formal schooling he was, in his own words, 'reared on the Bible and Foxe's Book of Martyrs', and he learned to read and write fluently. From an early age he loved the sea, and like his father had a passion for Protestantism. Being driven from his home by Catholics would have given him an even greater aversion to proponents of that faith.

2

A Career at Sea

In Kent, the young Francis Drake was placed 'with a neighbouring pilot who, by daily exercise, hardened him to the sailor's labour with a little bark (small sailing ship), wherewith he sailed up and down the coast, guided ships in and out of harbours, and sometimes transported merchandise into France and Zeeland (a province of the south-west Netherland), where a civil war was raging between the Dutch and the Spanish army of occupation)'. Leather and cloth from Kent would be bartered for continental wine and canvas. 'This young man, being diligent and pliable, gave such testimony of his care and diligence to the old pilot, that he dying issueless, in his will bequeathed, as a legacy, the bark to him, wherewith Drake having gathered a pretty sum of money, and receiving intelligence that John Hawkins made preparation of certain ships at Plymouth, for the voyage of America, which was called the New World, he made sale of his bark and, accompanied with certain brave and able mariners, he left Kent, and joined his labours and fortunes with Hawkins'. This was a reference to the 'Hawkins' family who were kinsmen (distant relatives) of the Drakes.[1]

'Olde William Haukins' of Plymouth was a man esteemed for his 'wisedome, valure, experience, and skill in sea...'. Beloved of King Henry VIII, he was 'one of the principall Sea-captaines in the West parts of England in his time'. Not content with the short voyages commonly only then made to the 'knowne coasts of Europe', Hawkins 'made three long and famous voyages unto the coast of Brasil', in a 'goodly ship of his owne of the burthen of 250 tunnes, called the *Paule of Plimouth*'. In the course of these voyages, he, 'traffiqued with the Negros' of Guinea', and 'took of them Elephants teeth, and other commodities which that place yeeldeth...'. Then, having crossed the Atlantic and arrived on the coast of Brazil, 'he grew into great familiarity and friendship' with her peoples, 'so much so that one of the savage kings' of that country allowed himself to be transported back to England; one Martin Cockeram of Plymouth being left behind as surety for his safety.[2]

In London, this King of Brazil was introduced to King Henry VIII, and at the sight of him, Henry and 'all the Nobilitie did not a little marvaile (marvel)...' for in the King's cheeks 'were holes made according to their savage manner', from which small bones protruded, being in his owne country a sign 'of a great braverie'. Such was the Brazilians' belief in the integrity of Hawkins and his men, that when their king died at sea on the return journey, Martin Cockeram was released 'without any harme to him'. It was thanks to William Hawkins that objects hitherto rarely seen, such as coconuts, oranges, bananas and African carvings became common sights in Plymouth.

William Hawkins died in 1554. He had two sons; the elder, also William, becoming Plymouth's premier ship owner with thirteen vessels. William junior would serve the city as mayor no less than three times; but his most important role was as overseer for the government of the West Country's maritime affairs. Although he had travelled as far as Brazil with his father, William preferred a life ashore, keeping accounts and doing inventories. Brother John however, who was twelve years younger, preferred a life at sea. His association with Francis Drake was soon to have profound consequences for their country, but meanwhile John would establish himself in his own right.

Born in Plymouth in 1532, John Hawkins was eight years older than Drake. In about 1559, he married Katherine, daughter of Benjamin Gonson, treasurer of the navy. Having 'made divers voyages to the Iles of the Canaries, and there by his good and upright dealing being growen in love and favour' with their peoples, Hawkins, 'made diligent inquisition (enquiry)' as to the prospects of trade in 'West India (the West Indies)'. Hawkins was now to pave the way for further expeditions in which he and Francis Drake would soon participate.[3]

The empire of Spain included possessions in the Far East, Europe and the Americas. Following Christopher Columbus's discovery of the West Indian islands between 1492 and 1504, Spain had developed her western empire, first by colonising the four largest West Indian islands and then extending to the north-west coast of South America, the so-called 'Spanish Main' (mainland). From here she took control of the Isthmus of Panama, where less than one hundred miles separates the Atlantic and Pacific Oceans, and then conquered the Aztec empire of Mexico, which was renamed 'New Spain'.

Moving southwards, she then conquered Peru and the west coast of Chile, from whose rich mines gold and silver were shipped northwards to the west coast of Panama, then carried by mule-train across the Isthmus to the port of Nombre de Dios ('name of God'). Twice a year the 'treasure fleet' arrived here from Spain to deliver provisions such as food, clothing, wine, oil and tools, and then carry the precious metals back to Spain. An alternative route was to sail southwards from Peru, but the Straits of Magellan were considered too dangerous to be used as a regular trade route.

∞

Having been assured 'that Negros were very good marchandise in Hispaniola (now Haiti/Dominican Republic)', and that they 'might easily bee had upon the coast of Guinea...', Hawkins made this knowlege known to friends of his in London, all of whom 'liked so well of his intention, that they became liberall contributors and adventurers in the action'.

The Indies (now West Indies) were given their name by Christopher Columbus who, having voyaged in 1492 from Spain to the Bahamas, Cuba and Hispaniola, mistakenly believed that he had reached India. For the same reason, the native people of the region were called 'Indians'.

Sir John Hawkins, by Custodis.
Photo: National Trust.

17

The irksome climate of the Indies took its toll of those of European stock, and the indigenous Indians fought to the death against enslavement. Hence the demand began for the African negro, who was found to be more resilient and compliant when set to work in the mines and plantations. Swift to recognise the profitability of the slave trade, royal courtiers, wealthy merchants, and government and naval officials came forward, anxious to invest in this booming business. The outcome was that in October 1562, Hawkins sailed in a fleet of three ships, himself as 'Generall' in command of the 120 ton *Salomon*.

In Sierra Leone, on the west coast of Africa, he obtained, 'partly by the sworde, and partly by other meanes', 300 negroes. 'With this praye (prey)' and other merchandise, he then crossed the Atlantic to the Island of Hispaniola where, at its various ports on the island, he was able to sell all of them. In exchange for the negroes, he received hides, ginger, sugars, and 'some quantitie of pearles', sufficient to fill not only his own three ships, but also two other hulks, which he 'sent into Spaine (to be traded)'. After this successful venture, Hawkins returned to England in September 1563. Nevertheless, he trusted the Spaniards 'no further, then that by his owne strength he was able still to master them', and in this he was soon to be proved right.

༄

One of the sponsors of Hawkins' second expedition to the West Indies of 1564 was Queen Elizabeth I, who provided him with his flagship, the 700 ton *Jesus of Lubeck*. This ship, now a veteran, had been purchased from the German Baltic port of Lubeck in the reign of Henry VIII. Henry Herbert, the 2nd Earl of Pembroke, and Lord Robert Dudley sailed with the fleet, which included three smaller ships and a total of 170 men.

They left Plymouth on October 18, 1564, and reached the coast of Africa in late December, having stopped briefly at Tenerife. The first attempt to capture negroes was met with stout resistance, but by the time they left Sierra Leone on January 29, 1565, they had on board 'a great company' of them.

Unfavourable winds meant that it was not until March 9 that they reached Dominica, where they were able to find desperately needed water. At Burburata on the Venezuelan coast, Hawkins discovered that

Spain's prohibition of foreign trade with her colonies was now being strictly enforced, and he was obliged to land a hundred well-armed men in order to persuade the Governor to comply. When the same problem arose at Rio de la Hacha on the Spanish Main (mainland), Hawkins landed 'one hundred men in armour', with two cannon; the result was that within ten days, the entire cargo of negroes was disposed of.

Hawkins arrived in the north Cornish port of Padstow on September 20. The voyage had been as 'profitable to the venturers, as also to the whole realm, in bringing home both gold, silver, pearls, and other jewels great store'. Soon it would be the turn of Francis Drake to fulfil his ambition and join his kinsman Hawkins on the high seas.

෴

At the age of eighteen, it is recorded that Drake was made Purser 'of a ship (voyaging) to Biscay'. In the autumn of 1564, he sold his boat and with two of his brothers and a number of friends, left Kent and returned to Plymouth, but only to find that Hawkins had already left on another expedition, which would be a virtual repetition of the first.

While he awaited Hawkins' return, Drake found employment with the Hawkins fleet, and took the opportunity to sail on November 9, 1566, with Captain John Lovell, an employee of Hawkins, on an expedition to the Indies. At Cape Verde, five hundred miles out in the Atlantic to the west of Senegal, Lovell captured some Portuguese slaving ships, along with their cargo of negro slaves; on the high seas, such vessels were considered fair game. Lovell then sailed on to Rio de la Hacha, where the Spanish governor, Miguel de Castellanos, tricked him into landing ninety slaves and then refused to pay for them.

After this debacle Hawkins did not employ Lovell again; for his part Drake realised that the Spaniards were not to be trusted.

෴

Drake is described as being 'Low of stature, of strong limbs, broade breasted, round headed...' and 'full bearded'. He had 'browne hayre', and his eyes were 'round, large and cleare'. As for his demeanour, he was 'well favoured, fayre, and of a cheerful countenance'.

Even in his formative years of seafaring, Drake regarded himself as an instrument of God's purpose and demonstrated his religious zeal on the voyage with Lovell, when he converted a Welsh crew-member from Roman Catholicism. One may ask why Drake, as a Protestant did not abhor slavery; the answer is that the negroes were considered to be heathens, and enslaving them was not therefore viewed as a moral offence.

∽

Drake was now to have his chance when, on October 2, 1567, a 'slaving fleet' of seven vessels and four hundred men sailed from Plymouth with John Hawkins in command, once again in the 700 ton *Jesus of Lubeck*, provided by the Queen. She was armed with 22 large guns and 42 smaller ones. Her Majesty also provided the 350 ton *Minion* (Captained by Thomas Hampton), and the remaining five ships were provided by Hawkins himself, who chose the twenty-five-year-old Francis Drake, now sturdy, and with reddish hair and beard, to command the 50 ton bark, *Judith*. Hawkins would now teach Drake the art of becoming an entrepreneur, or at least that was the idea!

At the Cape Verde Islands (in the Atlantic off Senegal), said Hawkins, they got but few negroes, at the price of 'great hurt and damage to our men'. This was chiefly on account of the opposition's 'envenomed arrowes', which at first seemed innocuous enough, 'yet there hardly escaped any that had blood drawen of them...'. Hawkins' men died in a strange sort of way, 'with their mouthes shut some tenne dayes before they died, and after their wounds were whole (had healed)'. The symptoms described correlate with those now known to be caused by tetanus. Hawkins himself suffered such a wound, but was fortunate enough to survive.[1]

By the time they left neighbouring Guinea, Hawkins, notwithstanding these setbacks, had acquired some 150 negroes. Then an assault on 'a towne of the Negros' boosted that number to between 400 and 500, but not before sixty or so of Hawkins' men had been killed in skirmishes. On February 3, having taken on water, they set sail yet again across the Atlantic and sighted the island of Dominica on March 27.

Here in the West Indies, despite the fact that King Philip of Spain had forbidden all local governors from dealing with unlicensed traders, nevertheless they had 'reasonable trade, and courteous entertainment' wherever they went, from the Island of Margarita (Venezuela) to Cartagena (Colombia).

The only place not to offer trade and hospitality was Rio de la Hacha, 'from whence come all the pearles', and its treasurer declined even to allow them to take on water. Hawkins was left with no choice but to enter the town by force, which he did with the loss of only two of his men, 'and no hurt done to the Spaniards', because after a volley of shots was fired at them, they fled. Hawkins then managed to trade secretly with the treasurer, who met with him one night and purchased from him 200 negroes. At Cartagena, however, the governor proved uncooperative so, as their trade was 'neere finished', they sailed on towards the coast of Florida.

When the *Jesus of Lubeck* was seriously damaged by a storm which caused her to leak badly, the fleet was 'inforced to take for our succour the Port which serveth the citie of Mexico (two hundred miles distant) called Saint John (San Juan) de Ulua'. On the way there, Hawkins captured three Spanish ships carrying a large number of people.

They entered the port on September 16, to discover twelve ships, reputed to contain £200,000 worth of gold and silver. However, Hawkins set these ships at liberty, without taking from them 'the weight of a groat (English silver coin worth 4 pence)...', as he was anxious to repair and revictual, and set sail once more. He also released the passengers from the three ships he had previously captured. He did, however, keep 'two men of estimation' (presumably noblemen) as hostages.

Hawkins knew that the Spanish treasure fleet was due to arrive at any time, and in order that 'there might no cause of quarrell rise betweene us', he sent a message to the Presidents of the Council in Mexico to explain his position. Sure enough, the following morning, September 17, thirteen great ships arrived at the mouth of the haven, which Hawkins understood to be 'the fleete of Spaine'. He accordingly sent message to the 'Generall' of that fleet to say that before he would permit it to enter the port, there had to be 'some order of conditions passe betweene us for our safe being there...'.

The Port of San Juan de Ulua was protected, in Hawkins' words, by 'a little Iland of stones not three foote above the water in the highest place...', standing but 'two bow shootes' from the mainland. 'Because the North wind hath there such violence', a ship must moor with its anchor fastened upon this island, or there would be 'no remedie... but death'.

Hawkins was now in a dilemma. He could permit the Spanish fleet, estimated value £1,800,000, to enter the port and risk 'their accustomed treason, which they never faile to execute, where they may have opportunitie', or he could keep them out, in which case it was quite likely that they would be shipwrecked. Fearful of provoking Queen Elizabeth's indignation in 'so waightie a matter' (after all, England and Spain were not then at war), Hawkins chose the former course of action.

Hawkins' messenger then returned to say that no less a person than the Viceroy of the Province of Mexico had arrived, and was anxious to see Hawkins' 'conditions'. Hawkins replied that he required victuals, which he would pay for, and a licence to sell as much ware as might furnish his wants. He also demanded that twelve gentlemen be exchanged by both parties, 'for the maintenance of peace', and that he be permitted to remain in possession of the island with its eleven peeces of ordnance, during their stay there.

Having agreed a compromise on ten hostages instead of twelve, the Viceroy replied with a letter of agreement, 'signed with his hande and sealed with his seale'. The matter had taken three days to resolve and now the Spanish fleet entered port.

There was little room in the harbour, and when a large vessel of 900 tons moored alongside Captain Hampton's *Minion*, Hawkins suspected that a great number of men were hiding in it and waiting to attack. He accordingly sent the Master of the *Judith* (commanded by Drake), who spoke Spanish, to the Viceroy to complain, whereupon the Viceroy detained the Master and blew a trumpet. This was the signal for the Spaniards to set upon the English from all sides. Those on the island fled, seeking to 'recover succour of the ships', but the Spaniard landed 'in multitudes' and slew all the Englishmen who were ashore without mercy, though a few of them escaped by coming aboard the *Jesus*.

Hawkins' fears were fully realised as three hundred men from the large vessel 'fell aboord the *Minion*'. Captain Hampton, however, had foreseen the event. He cut his ship's bow cables, and by 'hayling (hauling) away by the sternefastes' he got her out of the harbour.

The Spaniards now turned on the *Jesus*, which was successfully defended despite the loss of many men, and she managed to escape in the same manner as the *Minion*. Now, with the opposing vessels only two ships' lengths apart, the fight became intense. Within an hour the Admiral ('Admiral' being a term used to denote not only the commander of a fleet, but also his flagship) of the Spaniards was sunk, their vice admiral burned, and another of their principal ships also sunk. Thereafter, said Hawkins, the enemy was 'little able to annoy us'.

Meanwhile on the island, the Spaniards, who now had the English ordnance in their hands, made full use of it to sink the small ships, and to cut the masts and yards of the *Jesus*, rendering her unseaworthy. Hawkins now decided to bring the *Jesus* alongside the *Minion* to shelter the latter from the land batteries. The Spaniards then countered by firing two great ships and sailing them directly towards them. As Hawkins, with some difficulty, came aboard the *Minion* from the *Jesus*, her crew without further ado 'cut (hoisted) their sails'. The *Minion* then escaped, leaving the *Jesus* with her estimated treasure worth £100,000 behind. Those left alive from the *Jesus* followed the *Minion* in a small boat; others not so fortunate 'were forced to abide the mercy of the Spaniards'.

The only other ship to escape was Francis Drake's *Judith*. In his account of the voyage Hawkins does not mention his young kinsman by name, but states regretfully, that after the escape from San Juan de Ulua, the 'bark (Drake's) the same night forsooke us in our great miserie'. What explanation can there be for this? Were the ships separated in a storm? Hawkins makes no mention of one. There was no doubt that the expedition had been a disaster, and that no profit could possibly come from it. Did this debacle, both military and financial, cause Drake to lose confidence in his Admiral? Did he actually despise Hawkins for transforming a strong position into a weak one? Or did Drake simply panic? After all, this was his first command, and for one so young and inexperienced to suddenly find himself part of an inferior force in a confined space, pitted against the maritime might of Spain in a situation which was not of his choosing, must have been the ultimate nightmare! Drake gave no satisfactory answer as to why he acted in this way; but 'being his own man' was a trait which would mark him out in the future.

Drake brought his *Judith* and her crew of 65 safely back to Plymouth, by way of Mount's Bay in Cornwall which he reached on January 20, 1568. Hawkins, on the other hand, set sail with 'a great number of men and little victuals...'. After fourteen days at sea, hunger forced him to 'seek the land' where the men caught 'rats, cats, mice and dogs...', and purchased 'parrats and monkeyes', which they considered 'very profitable if they served the turne one dinner'.

Finally, on October 8, Hawkins' *Minion* reached the southern end of the 'bay (Gulf) of Mexico (near Panuco)', but 'found neither people, victuall, nor haven of reliefe...'. The men then divided themselves into two groups, those who, 'being forced with hunger,' begged to be set on land, and those who were 'desirous to goe homewardes'. Then, having taken on water, they set sail across the ocean for home.

Three days of storms were followed by a spell of fair weather. However, as time went by the men, being 'oppressed with famine', died continually; those that were left 'grew into such weaknesse' that they were hardly able to man the ship. Unfavourable winds then forced them to put in at the Spanish port of Vigo, where more men died having consumed an excess of fresh meat. However, with the help of some other ships and 'twelve fresh men', they set off once more and reached Mount's Bay in Cornwall on January 25, five days after Drake. By now, only fifteen of Hawkins's crewmen were left alive.

A hideous fate awaited the Englishmen whom Hawkins had put ashore, as the very few who ever returned home would testify. Those who survived attacks by local Indians were forced to surrender to the Spanish authorities, to be tried by the Spanish Inquisition (tribunal for the punishment of heresy or unbelief). Two were condemned to death, and the others were given two hundred lashes apiece and made to serve in the galleys for a period of eight years, after which time they would be permanently crippled. One, whom Drake especially remembered, was his cousin, Robert Barret of Saltash, who had been sent as messenger to the Spanish flagship. Barret refused to recant his Protestant faith and was burned alive on a pile of faggots in the market place at Seville. Another, Job Hortrop, who did live to tell the tale having been put ashore by Hawkins and captured by the Spaniards, endured eight years of imprisonment, twelve years of service as a galley slave, and another three years as a menial servant, before finally returning to England.

As news such as this spread throughout England, so hatred for Spain grew.

Queen Elizabeth's Court of Admiralty held an investigation into the happenings at San Juan de Ulua, and although numerous witnesses were called to give evidence, Drake was not one of them. Hawkins had hoped to mount an expedition to rescue his comrades stranded on the Mexican coast, but having possessed himself of a fortune and then lost both it, and the Queen's ship *Jesus of Lubeck*, this was forbidden to him.

∽

In November 1568, four Spanish ships sought refuge in English ports from French Huguenot (Protestant) pirates operating out of La Rochelle; three in Plymouth and one in Southampton. They carried a cargo of 800,000 ducats; money lent to the King of Spain by Genoese bankers with which the Duke of Alva in the Netherlands intended to pay his troops.

Elizabeth decided to have the money moved to the Tower of London 'for safety', and on learning of Hawkins' maltreatment by the Spaniards at San Juan de Ulua, was disinclined to return it. Spain reacted with a trade embargo, arresting English ships in Spanish ports and confiscating their cargoes. Now it was tit for tat, and henceforward any Spanish ship entering the English Channel did so at its peril! Many were subsequently captured, both by English privateers and by Dutch 'Sea Beggars' (patriotic Dutchmen who had escaped to England) whom Elizabeth tacitly allowed to operate from English ports. The Spanish trade embargo was to last until 1574.

∽

Drake's feelings after St Juan de Ulua can only be guessed at. He may have felt sorry for his commander, John Hawkins; or he may have been angry with him for trusting the Spaniards, who regarded the English as heathen people to whom promises made were not binding. In any event he had shown great skill in extricating his ship from a dangerous situation.

What Hawkins' precise orders to Drake had been were not known. However, the fleet having sailed under Hawkins' command, the ships would normally have been expected to accompany each other on the return journey. Hawkins' allegation that Drake had forsaken him was tantamount to an accusation of cowardice. It would have stung Drake, and struck at the very heart of his psyche - his sense of pride and self-respect. From now on, he would have something to prove!

Thereafter, Drake hated and detested the Spaniards, whom he blamed for putting him in a position where his reputation had been tarnished. Drake had now been 'blooded' as it were. He had felt the full heat of a close-quarter battle, fought in the most adverse of circumstances, neither of his choosing nor making, and yet he had managed to extricate himself, and save both his ship and his men.

The episode at San Juan de Ulua marked a turning point, both for John Hawkins and for Francis Drake. For Hawkins, the voyage had been a disaster, with no less than ten ships (including the five captured prizes) and £100,000 worth of treasure being lost. Drake, however, was under no such constraints. From now on it would be unrealistic to expect to trade peacefully with the Spanish Indies. He would embark on a career of piracy and plunder, and would not stop until he had collected the two million pounds which his cousin (John) Hawkins had lost (as his commander at San Juan de Ulua). He would avoid, if possible, close-quarter battles with the enemy, and instead use hit-and-run tactics and fight from long range.

But first there was a domestic matter to attend to! On June 4, 1569, Drake married Mary Newman, a Cornish lass of whom little is known, in Plymouth's Parish Church of St Budeaux, which lay near the River Tamar. For the next decade, however, he would spend precious little time ashore.

Late in 1570 Drake sailed from Plymouth in the 25 ton *Swan*, and by the spring of 1571 he had reached the Indies. This for Drake was a reconnaissance mission, and his objectives were twofold: to identify the route taken by the Spaniards in transporting their gold and to find a safe anchorage where he could lie low, both before and after intercepting and capturing it.

Church of St Budeaux, Plymouth.

26

The way the Spanards brought their treasure from South America to Spain was as follows. The Spanish Pacific fleet travelled northwards bringing gold and silver to Panama. From here it was transported by mule train across the Isthmus to the Caribbean port of Nombre de Dios to be taken back to Spain by the Atlantic fleet.

West of the town of Nombre de Dios, the River Chagres flowed into the Atlantic Ocean. In wintertime this river was full, and therefore navigable as far as the Spanish station of Venta Cruces, which was surrounded by hills and rain-soaked forests, and lay on the mule train route. In these hills lived the Cimaroons, negro slaves numbering two or three thousand, who had escaped from their Spanish masters and were now their sworn enemies.

∽

Something of the supreme confidence exhibited by Drake (then only thirty-one) in his dealings with the Spaniards, can be gleaned from a message he left nailed to the mast of a plundered Spanish ship. 'Captain, and others of this ship, we are surprised that you ran from us in that fashion! We only wished to speak with you, and since you will not come courteously to talk with us, you will find your frigate spoiled, by your own fault; done by English, who are well-disposed if there be no cause to the contrary. If there be cause, we will be devils, rather than men'.[5]

By questioning the crews of Spanish ships which he captured, Drake learned all he needed to know about the route of the treasure traffic, and in a daring raid up the Rio Chagres, made in company with French pirates, he made contact with the Cimaroons, whom he knew would be sympathetic to his cause. Drake also discovered a natural harbour on the Isthmus coast, sheltered from the winds and deep enough for him to anchor his ships, which he christened 'Port Pheasant', 'by reason of the great store of those goodly fowls which he and his companions did then daily kill and feed on in that place'. Here were abundant freshwater streams, fish and fruit, and before leaving he buried some stores for future use. Everything pointed to Nombre de Dios, and Drake was determined that when he returned, this is where he would strike. Drake returned to Plymouth late in 1571, his vessels laden with gold and silver coins, and Spanish goods.

3

The Raid on Panama

By 1572, Drake, 'by his traffique and Pyracy', had gathered together a sufficient sum of money, and it was now his intention to recover the losses 'which he had received by the Spaniards (at San Juan de Ullua)'. Any doubts he may have entertained as to the legitimacy of this idea were quickly dispelled by a preacher in the navy, who 'easily persuaded him' that this was perfectly lawful.[1]

Therefore, to this end, Drake sailed on May 24, 1572 as captain of the 70 ton *Pasco* (flagship, or 'admiral') from Plymouth in company with the 25 ton *Swan*, captained by his brother, John. 47 men and boys, all volunteers, sailed aboard the *Pasco*, and 47 aboard the *Swan*. Among them was another of Drake's brothers, namely Joseph, and John Oxenham of Plymouth. They also took with them 'three dainty pinnaces made in Plymouth, taken asunder, all in pieces, and stowed aboard to be set up again as occasion served'.[2]

Having crossed the Atlantic, they returned to their supposedly secret hideway, Port Pheasant. On arrival, however, they saw smoke and, pinned to a tree above a smouldering fire which had been lit to draw their attention, a note addressed to Drake. It was from a John Garrett of Plymouth, who had anticipated their arrival, informing them that the Spaniards had recently visited Port Pheasant, and had dug up the stores which Drake had left there.

Undeterred, Drake built a log fort and began constructing the prefabricated pinnaces. Rowing boats of shallow draught, these vessels were ideal for the transportation of men and stores in shallow water. Then arrived a ship, commanded by James Ranse of Plymouth who, with his crew of thirty, agreed to join forces with Drake.

Sailing westwards along the coast of the Isthmus, they anchored at the Isle of Pines, a promontory to the east of Nombre de Dios harbour. Here they encountered two frigates being loaded with timber by negro slaves. Drake conveyed these negroes to the shore and set them free, in the hope that they might join their fellow countrymen, the Cimaroons.

Then, leaving Ranse with thirty men to guard the ships, Drake sailed in the pinnaces, and after a night of rowing, reached Nombre de Dios on July 29 before the dawn. Having captured the Spanish battery which commanded the town, Drake was then free to attack it simultaneously from two sides.

It was here that his trumpeter was killed, and Drake himself received a wound that almost cost him his life. It happened while his brother John, and John Oxenham were attempting, with sixteen men, to break into the King's treasure house to which captured Spanish prisoners had been forced to guide them. Drake was in the town's market place, covering the operation, when he tripped and fell in a pool of blood. He had been shot in the thigh.

The operation was immediately aborted, the prospect of the 'rich spoil' (gold and jewels) which they had hoped to find was abandoned, and the priority now for the men was to save their captain's life, for 'while they enjoyed his presence, and had him to command them, they might recover wealth sufficient; but if once they lost him, they should hardly be able to recover home'. In other words, they regarded Drake as their talisman and depended on him to see them safely back to England. Therefore, having given him a drink, 'wherewith he recovered himself', they 'bound his scarf about his leg, for the stopping of the blood', and persuaded him to go aboard ship with them so that the wound could be properly 'searched and dressed'.

So despite meticulous planning, the operation had been a failure; the huge pile of silver bars which, by their estimation, was 'seventy foot in length, ten foot in breadth, and twelve foot in height' (which Drake had declined in favour of a more valuable haul), remained where his men had found it in the Governor's house, as did whatever valuables were contained in the treasure house.

Captain Ranse decided to part company and make for home. Drake now sailed for Cartagena, capital city of the Spanish Main, where he captured two Spanish ships and some prisoners, whom he questioned and then released. This operation was a feint, designed to put the Spaniards off the scent, for he quickly doubled back to the Isthmus.

Drake was forced to sink the *Swan*, not having sufficient men to man both her, the *Pasco* and the pinnaces. This was a sad day for his brother John, her captain: so to console him, Drake made John captain of the *Pasco*.

In the Bight of Darien, between the Isthmus of Panama and the Spanish Main, Drake discovered another hidden-away cove, which they named Port Plenty, where a fortnight was spent erecting huts, resting, practising archery, hunting for hogs, playing bowls and skittles, and setting up a blacksmith's forge.

Drake then took two pinnaces eastwards, beyond Cartagena, and entered the River Magdalena, where he captured several Spanish coasters. Finally they returned to Port Pheasant, visiting Port Plenty on the way to construct 'several magazines or storehouses', which would stand them in good stead if the Spaniards were to discover Port Pheasant. Meanwhile John Drake had made contact with the Cimaroons who, knowing them to be enemies of the Spaniards, declared that they were 'ready to assist and favour his (Drake's) enterprises... to the uttermost'. On his return, however, he discovered that the *Pasco* had been damaged by a storm, so he was obliged to find a more sheltered anchorage for her off Cativas (Colombia).

For all Drake's meticulous planning, he now received a setback. When he asked the Cimaroons to show him 'the means which they had to furnish him with gold and silver', the reply was that the Spaniards did not, in those rainy months, 'carry their treasure by land', and would not do so for another five months.

Drake and his men now occupied themselves by bringing all the ship's guns ashore, and building a substantial fort and, with the help of the Cimaroons, two large houses for all the company. These 'houses' were constructed of poles, palmito (a small palm) boughs, and plantain leaves.

Leaving John Drake to complete the fort, the ever energetic Drake set out eastwards with the pinnaces, visiting an island to replenish his stores, capturing a bark and two frigates, and taking shelter when 'foul and tempestuous weather' descended. They were running short of victuals, which Drake thought might be obtained, 'without great resistance' at Rio de la Hacha or Curacao. When the company of one of the other pinnaces told Drake that although they would 'willingly follow him through the world', they could not see how their pinnace could endure the stormy seas, nor how they could survive so long a journey with only one gammon of bacon and thirty pound of biscuit for 18 men, which they were now reduced to. Drake replied that he himself was in an even worse position, having only one gammon and forty pound of biscuit for his 24 men. They must depend on God's Almighty providence, which 'never faileth them that trusteth in Him'.

Drake's prayers were answered because almost immediately they captured a large Spanish frigate, 'laden with victual'. He promised the Spanish prisoners from this ship that if they would show him where water and fresh victuals were to be found, he would give them 'liberty, and all their apparel'. Both sides kept to the bargain.

They had been away from the *Pasco* for over five weeks, and now fever broke out amongst the men. They returned to their fort near Cativas, only to find that Drake's brother, John, and a young man called Richard Allen, had been killed only two days after their departure, whilst attempting to board a frigate.

By January 3, six men had contracted the fever, most of whom died within two or three days. When Drake's other brother, Joseph, died in his arms from the same cause, Drake, in order to discover the cause, ordered a post mortem. The surgeon found the liver swollen, the heart 'sodden', and the guts 'all fair'. Then came the news that they had been waiting for; from the Cimaroons they learnt that the Spanish fleet had arrived in Nombre de Dios.

This report was confirmed when a Spanish frigate was captured, aboard which were one woman and twelve men. These prisoners were 'used very courteously', and guarded from the Cimaroons who, to 'revenge the wrongs and injuries which the Spanish nation had done them', would willingly have cut their (the Spaniards') throats. Drake now conferred with his company and with the 'chiefest of the Cimaroons' as to what the plan of action should be. In the meantime he was hampered by the fact that by February 3, no less than 28 of his men had died of the fever.

Drake now departed, leaving Ellis Hixom who, in his pinnace *Lion*, had captured the Spanish frigate, to 'keep the ship... tend the sick, and guard the prisoners'. His party numbered 48, of which only 18 were Englishmen, the remainder being Cimaroons, four of whom went on ahead as scouts. They carried arms, and sufficient victuals for a long march, and whenever they stopped, the Cimaroons, true to form, constructed houses to shelter them. The Cimaroons did not have priests as such. Drake taught them the Lord's Prayer, and instructed them 'in some measure concerning God's true worship'.

After four days they came to a high hill, on which stood a tree into which the Cimaroons had cut steps to facilitate the ascent to the top, where they had made a platform ('bower') on which as many as twelve men could be seated. From this vantage point, not only could the Atlantic Ocean be seen, but also the Pacific (which they knew as the 'South Atlantic'). Having seen this view, Drake 'besought Almighty God of His goodness to give him life and leave to sail once in an English ship in that sea'.[3] Another three days of marching brought them to within sight of Panama, where ships could be seen 'riding in the road'. Certain chosen Cimaroons, clothed in the same apparel as the local negroes, were then sent into the town as spies.

They returned with the news that the Treasurer of Lima, who was en route to Spain, proposed that very night to travel with the mule train to Nombre de Dios, and that of his 14 mules, 8 would be laden with gold and another with jewels. Also the spies had learnt that the following night, another two mule trains would set forth carrying victuals and a quantity of silver.

They now marched inland, towards the town of Venta Cruz, and on the way captured a Spanish soldier who, in return for not being handed over to the Cimaroons, who would undoubtedly have killed him, promised to ensure that that night, they should have 'more gold, besided jewels and pearls of great price, than all they could carry'.

The ambush was duly prepared, and when night fell, a deep-sounding bell was heard which heralded the arrival of the mule train. However, on this occasion, the reckless behaviour of one of Drake's men, a Robert Pike, who was the worse for drink, accidentally alerted the Spaniards, depriving Drake and his men of 'a most rich booty'. It was now necessary to retreat, before retribution followed.

In a wood on the outskirts of Venta Cruz, they encountered a company of Spanish soldiers, who fired at them, killing one man and wounding several others including Drake himself. They replied with 'shot and arrows', before the Cimaroons charged out of the thickets, forcing the soldiers to flee.

In Venta Cruz, a town of 40 or 50 houses, were three 'gentlewomen' who had recently been 'delivered of children'. Drake, who had previously instructed those men in his company that they 'should never hurt any woman', nor any man 'that had not weapon in his hand', sent word to these women that no wrong would be done to them. The women made it clear, however, that they would only be satisfied if Drake gave them this reassurance in person. This he did.

The Cimaroons were anxious to give Drake and his men hospitality, and to provide food for them, but Drake, who had been away from his ship for almost a fortnight, was anxious about the sick men aboard whom he had left behind. They therefore returned, marching for 'many days with hungry stomachs'. Back on board his ship, Drake now informed the company that he intended to repeat the journey to Panama, and this time those who had been left behind, and who had now recovered their health and strength, could accompany him.

Having listened to the opinions of both his men and the Cimaroons, Drake sent John Oxenham eastwards in the pinnace *Bear* to Tolu (Colombia, near Nombre de Dios) in search of food, while he himself sailed westward in the *Minion* towards Cabezas (Nicaragua), in the hope of intercepting vessels carrying treasure from Veragua and Nicaragua to the fleet. Although Drake was unsuccessful, not so Oxenham, who captured and commandeered a frigate containing a welcome quantity of maize, hogs and hens.

Next day the *Minion*, *Bear*, and newly acquired 'frigate of Tolu' returned to Cativas, where they encountered a French ship captained by Guillaume de Testu, a Huguenot privateer. Having exchanged gifts, and provided de Testu with some desperately needed water, Drake learnt from the Frenchman of the massacre in Paris of Protestants, which had occurred six months previously, on St Bartholomew's Day.

It was now decided that 20 of de Testu's men, and 15 of Drake's, together with the Cimaroons, would man the frigate and two pinnaces (the pinnace *Lion* having previously been deliberately sunk as Drake had not the men to man her), and, leaving the ships behind, sail towards Rio Francisco. Because of a shortage of water they were obliged to leave the frigate, which was manned by a combined English and French crew, at Cabezas.

Having landed at Rio Francisco, they set out for the road which linked Panama with Nombre de Dios, and on the morning of April 1, they heard the bells which heralded the arrival of a mule train. In fact there were three trains (or 'recoes', as the Spaniards called them; this being their word for a drove of beasts of burden), which between them carried three hundred pounds weight of silver. Drake's men grabbed the heads of the foremost and hindmost mules, wherupon the remainder 'stayed and laid down, as their manner is'.

In the exchange of bullets and arrows, one of the Cimaroons was killed and de Testu was 'sore wounded with hail shot in the belly'. Having seen off the Spanish guard, Drake's men, being weary, contented themslves with a few bars and quoits (rings) of gold, then buried about 15 tons of silver in the bed of a shallow river, under fallen trees, and in burrows which 'great land-crabs' had made in the earth.

De Testu's wound forced Drake to leave him behind, in the care of two of his French soldiers. Another Frenchman went missing; they later discovered that he had drunk too much wine, become lost in the woods and, having been captured and tortured by the Spaniards, revealed to them the place of the buried treasure.

Having marched for two days towards Rio Francisco to rendezvous with their pinnaces, they encountered instead seven Spanish pinnaces, which had been searching for them. The fear now was that Drake's men had been captured, tortured, and revealed the whereabouts of the ships that were to carry them home.

Strong winds now forced the Spaniards to sail away, but also prevented the English pinnaces from keeping their appointment with Drake. He therefore suggested that they construct a raft, using wood from trees brought down river by a recent storm. 'I will be one (to volunteer)', said Drake, 'who will be the other?'

The raft was duly made, a 'biscuit sack' serving as its sail, and a young tree shaped to form a rudder. As Drake departed, in company with his crewman, John Smith, two Frenchmen 'that could swim very well', and some Cimaroons, he promised that if it pleased God to return him safely to his frigate, then by one means or another, he would return and 'get them (the remainder) all aboard, in despite of all the Spaniards in the Indies'.

After six hours spent sitting in the raft up to their waists in water, they sighted the pinnaces, which failed to see them and instead of coming to the rescue, took cover for the night behind a headland. Drake then came ashore and ran to join them and acquaint them with what had happened.

That night, Drake, true to his word, rowed to Rio Francisco and rescued his men and what treasure they had managed to acquire. Then, having arrived back aboard his ship, he divided it equally between the French and the English.

A fortnight later they set sail again, Drake in the meantime having secretly arranged with the Cimaroons (i.e. without the knowledge of the

French) that 12 of his men and 16 of theirs should make another voyage with the object of rescuing de Testu and recovering the treasure. This was one of the rare occasions when Drake was overruled. Concerned for his safety, his men were adamant that they 'would by no means... condescend' for him 'to suffer to adventure again this time...', so the task was assigned to John Oxenham and Thomas Sherwell. Drake was permitted by his men to row them to Rio Francisco and set them ashore, and in doing so they rescued one of the two Frenchmen who had been left with de Testu.

The Frenchman told them that within half an hour of their departing, the Spaniards had captured de Testu and the other Frenchman. He himself had escaped. He believed that the Spaniards had employed nearly 2000 of their own people and negroes to dig and locate the treasure which Drake had hidden. Notwithstanding this bad news, Drake's party pressed on, and managed to find 13 bars of silver and 'some few quoits of gold', which had remained undiscovered.

They now set sail for home, the French ship accompanying them only as far as San Bernado (island off Colombia). In a gesture of defiance, they sailed close to Cartagena and deliberately within sight of the Spanish fleet (which was assembled ready to set sail for Spain), with the flag of St George flying from the main top, and silk streamers and 'ancients' (ensigns) trailing down to the water.

In the small hours of the morning they captured a frigate laden with maize, hens, and some most welcome honey. The Spanish crew was set ashore, but their ship was pressed into service. (Unlike the Spanish, it was neither the policy of Drake nor that of his countrymen to enslave prisoners whom they had captured.) Five days later they anchored at Cabezas, where they careened both ships and 'new tallowed' them (protected their hulls with grease). The pinnaces, being of no further use, were burned, their ironwork being given to the Cimaroons.

Now it was time to say goodbye to the Cimaroons. Drake invited them to choose objects which they liked from the frigates, sought out linen and silks for their wives, and donated to Pedro, the chief of them, a scimitar which de Testu had given to him. Then, with 'good love and liking', they set sail for Cape San Antonio (Cuba), where they found a great store of turtles' eggs, and caught no less than 250 turtles during the night, some of which they dried and preserved.

Some 200 frigates plied regularly between Cartagena and Nombre de

Dios, and during their 'abode in those parts', they captured most of them, some on more than one occasion. However, none were ever burnt or sunk, unless they acted like men-of-war. As for the prisoners, no violence was offered to them, they were always 'secured from the rage of the Cimaroons', and either soon released, or kept aboard until the danger of the Spaniards discovering Drake's ships was past.

Heavy rains provided the water that they would otherwise have been obliged to obtain by stopping off at Newfoundland, so they were able to sail directly from Cape Florida to the Isles of Scilly, a journey of twenty-three days, and arrive at Plymouth 'about sermon time' on August 9, 1573. So speedily did the news of Drake's return 'pass over all the church', and 'surpass the mindss' of all the congregation with 'desire and delight', that everyone rushed down to the sea front, 'very few or none' remaining with the preacher!

Drake had shown leadership and bravery, and his careful reconnaissance and meticulous planning had paid off, for this time the value of the haul (which included two Spanish vessels captured as prizes, and silver and gold from the mines of Peru) was estimated at about 100,000 pesos (£40,000). This was sufficient to make Drake a wealthy man, but the price had been high. The 25 ton *Swan* and three pinnaces had been lost, and more than half the crew were dead including two of Drake's brothers.

෴

It now appeared that there might be the possibility of a reconciliation and peace treaty between England and Spain. As it was not in Drake's nature to be idle, he decided to join the Royal Navy, fitted three ships out at his own expense, and sailed as captain of the *Falcon*. This was in support of a campaign led by Walter Devereaux, 1st Earl of Essex (whose seven-year-old son Robert would one day become a favourite of the Queen at her Court), aimed at suppressing the Irish, who were in rebellion against English rule. Drake's young cousin, John Drake, went with him and acted as his page.

Having arrived in Ireland at the end of 1574, Drake was given command of a naval force charged with the capture of the Island of Rathlin, off the north coast of Antrim where Essex intended to establish a fort. It was not until July 26 the following year that the island surrendered, and there followed a bloody massacre. As many as 500 people, women and children included, were put to the sword; though there is no evidence to link Drake personally with this genocide.

While in Ireland, Drake had met and made friends with Thomas Doughty, a soldier and courtier, who himself had friends in high places: amongst them Robert Dudley, Earl of Leicester, and William Cecil, Lord Burghley, who was the Queen's Chief Minister. Soon Doughty would accompany Drake on his circumnavigation of the world.

When his services were no longer required, Drake returned to England, with a letter from Essex to Sir Francis Walsingham, one of Queen Elizabeth's principal Secretaries of State, recommending him as a man most fitted to serve against the Spaniards. Drake's chance came when King Philip annoyed the Queen by seizing a ship belonging to Sir Thomas Osborne. Now, with the support of Leicester, and of Sir Christopher Hatton, Vice-Chamberlain and Privy Councillor, Drake was introduced to Her Majesty who informed him that she would 'gladly be revenged on the King of Spain' for the 'divers injuries' that she had received.[1] There would now be a subtle change in Drake's role, viz. from that of self-interested 'pirate', to that of 'privateer' (one who acts with the approval of his sovereign, in return for that sovereign's protection).

John Oxenham, Drake's companion on the voyage to Panama, did not fare so well. He sailed again to the Isthmus from Plymouth, only to be captured by the Spaniards. Neither he nor any of his companions ever returned home.

4

Elizabeth Succeeds to the Throne – Threats to Her Realm

In order fully to appreciate how Drake was able to play his increasingly important role upon the world's stage, it is first necessary to understand how the various European powers were aligned, in particular in regard to their economics, politics, and religion, and to the factors which led to this present alignment.

This was the dawn of the Elizabethan era, which would herald a great burgeoning of creative activity, with names like William Shakespeare, Edmund Spencer, William Byrd and Christopher Marlowe to the fore. In 1534, Henry VIII had freed himself from the clutches and inhibitory discipline of the Church of Rome, and his action was perhaps now being reflected in a similar release of inhibitions by the citizens of the English realm.

For although the western world was dominated by the great and powerful empire of Catholic Spain, it was as the loyal subject of the Protestant Queen Elizabeth – then the only Queen in the world of this religious persuasion – who had no empire of her own whatsoever, that Drake would demonstrate his genius!

Prior to Elizabeth's accession to the throne England was beset by an ongoing power struggle between its Catholic and Protestant factions. Although for a person such as Francis Drake, being at sea could be dangerous enough, being on land could be equally so, when the Tower, rack, and thumbscrew awaited those who for one reason or another, found themselves backing the wrong side in this era of endless plotting and treachery.

The progress of Elizabeth, Drake's future Queen whom he would one day serve with great distinction, was tortuous to say the least, and also fraught with danger. Henry VIII's break with Rome was a principal factor in shaping England's future relationship with its immediate neighbours, and with the continent of Europe; in particular with Spain, with whom war with England (a war in which Drake was to become heavily involved), loomed ever closer.

Elizabeth, the daughter of Henry VIII and his second wife, Anne Boleyn, was born at Greenwich Palace on September 7, 1533. Henry's propensity for marrying, and then disposing of his wives would have profound reper- cussions for his family. Elizabeth's own mother was executed, and of her five stepmothers, one also was executed, two had their marriages to Henry annulled, and two died in childbirth. Her own traumatic battle to succeed to the throne would shape her character, and teach her the virtues of prudence, endurance and healthy scepti- cism when it came to dealing with those around her.

Elizabeth I when Princess, artist unknown.
Photo: The Royal Collection ©2004 Her Majesty Queen Elizabeth II.

Henry's first wife, Catherine of Aragon, had failed to provide him with a male heir after twenty-four years of marriage, and by the late 1520s it was clear that she was past childbearing age. Henry was therefore anxious to be divorced from her, and was encouraged in this by Anne Boleyn (the daughter of wealthy London merchant Sir Thomas Boleyn), who had designs on Henry herself; but he knew that to marry her, he would require the special permission of the Pope.

In the spring of 1532, the English Catholic Church, in the face of a united King Henry and his Parliament, acceded to all of his demands: namely divorce from Catherine, marriage to Anne, the declaration that Mary (Henry's child by Catherine) was a bastard, and recognition for the unborn child of Henry's, which Anne was presently carrying. When she married Henry in the following year 1533, Anne was already six months pregnant with a daughter, Elizabeth.

In 1534, the 'Act of Supremacy' was passed, cementing the break with Rome and declaring the King of England (Henry) to be supreme head of the Church of England, (instead of the Pope). An 'Act of Succession' declared that Henry's only lawful heirs were his offspring by Anne Boleyn.

Elizabeth had fiery-red hair and a temper to match! A child protégé, she was eloquent in her native tongue, proficient in Latin, Greek, and Mathematics, and had a knowledge of French and Italian. She could shoot with a bow and arrow, create exquisite embroidery, and play a variety of musical instruments including the virginals (small harpsicord). Her young life, however, was highly problematical.

In May 1536, when Elizabeth was not yet three, her mother Anne Boleyn was beheaded for alleged multiple adultery and incest. Elizabeth was promptly rejected by her father; now it was her turn to be branded a bastard. She was banished from Court to Hatfield House in Hertfordshire, which from now on would be her principal residence. Mary, her half-sister, was also banished to Hatfield House, and was made Elizabeth's lady-in-waiting which, as the elder of the two, she bitterly resented.

Immediately after Anne Boleyn's execution, Henry married Jane Seymour, who had been one of Anne's ladies-in-waiting. On July 1, Parliament declared that both Mary Tudor, Henry VIII's daughter by his first wife (Catherine of Aragon), and Elizabeth, his daughter by his second wife (Anne Boleyn), were illegitimate, and it was to be a child born of the union of Henry to Queen Jane who would be the legitimate successor to the throne. Despite this however, it was for Henry himself to make the ultimate decision as to his evential successor.

On October 12, 1537, Jane Seymour, succeeding where her predecessors had failed, gave birth to a son, Edward but died twelve days later and was succeeded by Anne of Cleves. This marriage was never consummated, and when divorce followed, Catherine Howard, a maid of honour to Anne of Cleves, became Henry's fifth wife in July, 1540. Two years later Catherine was executed for adultery.

PROBLEMS WITH THE SCOTS.

The King of Scotland, James V, had two sons, both of whom died young, but on December 8, 1542, his Queen, Mary of Guise, bore him a daughter, Mary Stuart. In the same month, Henry VIII, determined to reassert England's dominance over his neighbour, had gone to war with the Scots, and routed them at the Battle of Solway Moss. On December 14, James V died and the crown of Scotland passed to the infant Mary Stuart, who was then only one week old.

∾

Catherine Parr, Henry's sixth wife whom he married in 1543, managed to effect a reconciliation between her husband and his two daughters, with the result that Mary and Elizabeth were brought back to Court and rehabilitated.

For all his destructiveness over the monasteries and their contents, it is Henry who must take credit for the foundation of the Royal Navy. The first naval dockyard was established at Portsmouth on the south coast in 1496. However, the distance from London proved inconvenient, so Henry VIII created three more royal dockyards: one at Deptford, another at Woolwich on the River Thames near Greenwich, and the third at Chatham (which had served as an anchorage up until 1570), on Kent's River Medway. Henry also broke with tradition by making it a requirement that the Lord High Admiral go to sea, instead of being a mere figurehead as had hitherto been the case.

To Henry VIII must also be attributed a new concept of naval warfare. Instead of attacking the enemy in line abreast (in a manner reminiscent of a land battle), and then ramming, grappling and boarding, the ships would 'stand off', and fire their heavy guns from a distance. Francis Drake would soon have cause to be grateful to King Henry VIII for this foresight, which would stand England in good stead in the years to come, and in particular, when war came with Spain.

EDWARD VI.

Henry VIII died on January 28, 1547, and was succeeded by his son, Edward VI. As Edward was a minor, aged only nine, his uncle, Edward Seymour, acted as his 'Protector'. (Seymour was subsequently to be deposed and executed for treason.) The following year, Mary Stuart, Queen of Scots, was sent to France, to be educated and cared for by the family of her mother, Mary of Guise, who remained in Scotland as regent.

Edward VI died on July 6, 1553, from tuberculosis. Four days later,

John Dudley, Duke of Northumberland, who had replaced Edward Seymour as the King's Protector, and whose son Lord Guildford Dudley had married Lady Jane Grey (a distant relative of Henry VIII), proclaimed Lady Jane Queen. However, Queen Jane was to reign for five days only because, supported not only by her sister Elizabeth but also by many of England's most powerful and influential families, Mary Tudor made a triumphal entry into London, where on July 19, she herself was proclaimed Queen. (Lady Jane Grey was subsequently executed, as was Guildford Dudley and his father John.)

MARY TUDOR.

Like her Spanish mother, Catherine of Aragon, Mary Tudor was a staunch Catholic, and her mission was to restore England to 'the true faith'. Edward VI's reign had seen a further dismantling of the English Catholic Church and its traditions. This was now reversed by Mary, who insisted that Roman Catholicism be practised throughout the land. Those who failed to comply were savagely persecuted. Mary Tudor wished her step-sister, Elizabeth, to adopt the Catholic faith, but Elizabeth was not to be persuaded.

Mary Tudor in 1544 when she was twenty-eight, by Master John.

Photo: National Portrait Gallery, London.

Holy Roman Emperor and King of Spain, Charles V, frustrated by his efforts to impose Catholicism on France, now hoped to exert his influence on England by marrying his eldest son and heir, Philip, then aged twenty-seven, to the thirty-eight-year-old Mary Tudor. Charles also realised that an Anglo-Spanish alliance, with control of Flanders, would also give him control of the

Channel and all its trade. When Mary Tudor declared her intention to marry Philip, there followed in January 1554 a rebellion in Kent (Francis Drake's county of adoption, since his family's expulsion from Devon) led by by Sir Thomas Wyatt who bitterly opposed such plans. The rebellion was unsuccessful.

Suspected of complicity in the Wyatt rebellion, with the idea of setting herself upon the throne, Elizabeth now faced a charge of treason, for which the penalty was hanging, drawing and quartering. Elizabeth was first confined to her apartments at Whitehall, and then on March 18, 1554, sent to the Tower (where her own mother, Anne Boleyn, had been imprisoned and executed); here she waited every minute of every day for that fateful knock on the door, which would spell her doom.

On April 11, 1554, Wyatt was executed, proclaiming with his final words that Elizabeth was innocent of all knowledge of his intended rebellion. Finally, on May 19, Elizabeth was released, only to be taken to Woodstock to remain in the custody of Sir Henry Bedingfield.

King Philip II of Spain, artist unknown.

Photo: National Portrait Gallery, London.

Elizabeth's troubles were not yet over, for in an attempt to prove her half-sister guilty of heresy, Mary asked her if she believed in transubstantiation (the literal transformation of communion bread and wine into the body and blood of Christ). Sensing a trap, Elizabeth replied disingenuously, 'His was the word that spake it, He took the bread and brake it, And what that word doth make it, I do believe and take it.'[1]

Philip duly set sail for England, landed at Southampton, and on July 25, 1554, was married to Mary Tudor in the great cathedral of Winchester. An English shilling minted at the time depicted busts of the couple facing one another, for which reason it became known as the 'kissing shilling'. The marriage, however, was deeply unpopular with the people of England, who saw their country being swallowed up by the great Empire of Spain.

Those who had supported Mary Tudor in her claim to the throne may not have realised just how ruthless a person she was, because in the years that were to follow 300 or so Protestant men, women and children would be burned alive at the stake; including the Protestant Bishops Thomas Cranmer, Hugh Latimer and Nicholas Ridley.

Philip's view of the English succession was as follows: he was anxious that Elizabeth, a Protestant, did not succeed to the throne; but he was even more loth to see Mary Stuart, Queen of Scots, as a future Queen of England (even though, as Henry VII's great-granddaughter, she was a strong claimant), the over-riding factor being that even though the latter was a Catholic, she was an ally of his arch-enemy, France.

Mary Tudor failed to conceive a child, her first pregnancy was a phantom, as was her second a year later. In September 1555, Philip lost interest in his country of adoption and in his wife, who had failed to provide him with an heir, and returned to Spain. The following year, his father Charles V abdicated, and he became King Philip II of Spain. Philip now became embroiled in a disastrous campaign against the French, which would eventually result in January, 1558, in England losing her last possession in France, namely Calais.

Mary Tudor, having become ill with dropsy (accumulation of fluid in the body), died at 7a.m. on November 17, 1558, aged forty-two, having only ten days previously finally agreed that Elizabeth should be her successor. A condition was that the Roman Catholic faith should be allowed to continue, to which Elizabeth concurred.

Mary Tudor was nicknamed 'Bloody Mary' because of her savage persecution of Protestants. However, in her favour was the fact that during her reign, she had kept the ships of the Royal Navy in good repair, the sum of £14,000 being put aside each year for this purpose.

Elizabeth was sitting in the Great Park at Hatfield under an oak tree, reading a book, when she heard the news. She fell on her knees and recited in Latin the words of Psalm 118 – 'This is the Lord's doing; it is marvelous in our eyes. This is the day that the Lord has made; let us rejoice and be glad in it.'[2] Six days later she moved to London and was crowned Queen on January 15, 1559, amidst huge rejoicings. By wearing her hair 'down' at her coronation, Elizabeth encouraged the image of herself as the 'virgin Queen'. Then aged twenty-four, she would go on to have many suitors, but it is doubtful whether any of her relationships were of a sexual nature. She would resist all attempts by her Privy Council to 'marry her off', because in her own words, she had already 'joined herself in marriage to an husband, namely the Kingdom of England'.[3] She was determined that this situation would pertain for the rest of her life. 'In the end,' she said, 'this shall be for me sufficient, that a marble stone shall declare that a Queen, having reigned such a time, lived and died a virgin.'[4]

It is ironic that, had Mary Tudor lived and remained married to Philip, then there would have been no occasion for Spain and England to go to war, and had they produced a child, then the Catholic succession would in all probability have been assured for future years. Hostilities might also have been avoided had Elizabeth not refused Philip's proposal of marriage, which the newly-widowed Spanish King made to the newly-crowned English Queen. However, Elizabeth declined him, and now England had a Protestant monarch on the throne. This, in Spanish eyes, was no less than a heresy, and from the time of Elizabeth's coronation it was inevitable that the two countries would become bitter enemies.

ELIZABETH AND HER COURT.

Elizabeth's perilous progression to the throne had left her with no illusions. Of her experience of life thus far, she would say, '... I see no such great cause why I should either be fond to live or fear to die. I have had good experience of this world, and I know what it is to be a subject and what to be a sovereign. Good neighbours I have had, and I have met with bad: and in trust I have found treason'[5] – truly the voice of an old head on young shoulders!

Elizabeth's accession to the English throne heralded, to begin with at any rate, a more tolerant era. As she was later to declare, she had no intention to 'inquire into men's consciences in matters of religion'. However, it was not to last and when all but one of her predecessor Mary Tudor's Catholic bishops refused to swear an oath of allegiance accepting Elizabeth as head of the new (Protestant) Church of England, they were imprisoned in the Tower.[6]

In choosing those who were to serve on her chief advisory body, the Privy Council, Elizabeth was scrupulously careful. A sound education, combined with wisdom and industriousness, were prerequisites, as epitomised by her Chief Secretary of State (and later Lord High Treasurer), Lord Burghley. A minority of Catholics were included; all that was necessary was for them to acknowledge her supremacy, but if they wished to celebrate the Mass, then they must do so in private.

MARY, QUEEN OF SCOTS.

Next in line to the throne of England was the Catholic Mary Stuart, daughter of James V of Scotland and Mary of Guise (of the noble French family of Lorraine) and great-granddaughter of King Henry VII. In Mary Stuart's eyes, Queen Elizabeth, being the product of what she regarded as the illegal marriage of Henry VIII to Anne Boleyn, was illegitimate.

In April, 1558, when she was sixteen, Mary Stuart had married the fourteen-year-old eldest son ('Dauphin') of King Henry II of France, in the Cathedral of Notre Dame in Paris. When, the follow-ing year, Henry II died, the Dauphin duly succeeded him as King Francis II, with Mary Stuart as his queen-consort. However, when in 1560, Francis II himself died, Mary Stuart decided to return to Scotland.

Mary, Queen of Scots, 1558, by François Clouet
Photo: The Royal Collection ©2004 Her Majesty Queen Elizabeth II.

In the November of that year, Mary Stuart laid claim to the throne of England, on the grounds that the present Queen, Elizabeth, was illegiti-mate, and that she, Mary, was the great-granddaughter of King Henry VII.

In 1565, against Elizabeth's wishes, Mary Stuart married her cousin, the twenty-year-old Henry Stuart, Lord Darnley, in the Chapel Royal at Holyrood Palace, in Edinburgh. The subsequent birth of their son, James, was viewed with dismay in England, where Elizabeth's Council had long been urging the Queen herself to marry and hopefully, to procreate.

Darnley however proved to be a drunkard, and within a year he was found murdered. Mary Stuart, who was suspected of complicity in the death of her late husband, was abducted, taken to Dunbar, and raped by the Earl of Bothwell, who believed that his action would force Mary into marrying him. In the event, he was right, for a fortnight later the couple were married. The result was predictable; the people of Scotland now saw their Queen not as a victimised mother, but as a whore. The Scottish nobles rose in revolt and Mary Stuart's forces were defeated at the Battle of Langside. Now pregnant with twins, she was imprisoned in the island fortress of Loch Leven in Fife, where she miscarried. She then abdicated in favour of her son James. Bothwell fled to Norway, never to return to Scotland.

In May 1568, after ten months of imprisonment, Mary Stuart escaped. Troops rushed to support her, but her forces were defeated and she was obliged to flee to England and throw herself at the mercy of Elizabeth. Having taken Mary Stuart into custody, Elizabeth was now faced with a dilemma; it would be folly to help restore Mary Stuart, a Catholic, and a friend of the French, to the throne of Scotland (officially a Protestant country since 1557).

In the same year, Philip II of Spain angered Elizabeth by dismissing, on religious grounds, her Ambassador to Madrid. By this time, Elizabeth was supporting the Protestants of the Spanish Netherlands (the Netherlands then included present-day Holland, Belgium and north-eastern France) in their resistance to Fernando Alvarez de Toledo, Duke of Alva, and his Spanish army of occupation. The Netherlands were of great strategic interest to both England and Spain, the city of Antwerp providing the largest export market for English wool, but the country also being a potential springboard for a Spanish invasion of England.

Mary Stuart, currently imprisoned in the bleak hilltop castle of Tutbury in Staffordshire, was now a potential rallying point for disaffected earls of Catholic persuasion in the north of England, in particular those of Westmorland and Northumberland.

Sure enough, at midnight on November 9, 1569, the northern earls rose in revolt, and the following day entered the fortress-city of Durham, broke into the cathedral, and in a gesture of defiance burned its Protestant bibles and prayer books. Realising that their aim was to release Mary Stuart, Elizabeth had her swiftly moved south from Tutbury, to Coventry in Warwickshire. She then sent a force to intercept the rebels who, faced with overwhelming odds, retreated. In the autumn of 1570, Mary Stuart was imprisoned at Sheffield, Yorkshire, where she remained under the guardianship of George Talbot, 6th Earl of Shrewsbury, for the next fourteen years.

RELIGIOUS STRIFE.

In 1570, Pope Pius V, encouraged by Philip of Spain, issued a Bull (edict) *Regnans in Excelsis*, which denounced Queen Elizabeth as a bastard and a heretic, denied her right to reign, and not only absolved her subjects from the need to show her allegiance, but actively encouraged anyone who was so minded to assassinate her. 'Whosoever sends her (Elizabeth) out of the world, with the pious intention of doing God's service,' said the Pope, 'not only does not sin, but gains merit.'

In Paris, on August 24, 1572, St Bartholomew's Day, Catholics fell upon their Protestant neighbours and massacred them. Many English Protestants took refuge in the home of the English Ambassador, Sir Francis Walsingham, who himself barely escaped with his life. This prompted Elizabeth to recall him and appoint him her Secretary of State, in which position he effectively became her chief intelligence-gatherer and spymaster.

A FRENCH ROMANCE.

A serious contender for Elizabeth's hand was Henry, Duke of Anjou, brother of King Henry III of France. Small in stature, and scarred by a previous attack of smallpox, he arrived in Greenwich on August 17, 1579 for an audience with the Queen. Elizabeth, then aged forty-five, promptly fell in love with Anjou, who was aged only twenty-four, nicknaming him fondly, 'The Frog'.

Elizabeth was anxious to have the support of her Privy Council for her proposed marriage but, to her disappointment, the Council was divided, not least because Anjou was a Catholic. In the face of such lukewarm support, she decided to abandon her matrimonial plans.

∾

Under an Act passed in 1581, it became treasonable for Catholics to withdraw from the Church of England, and on conviction for saying

Mass, they were liable for a heavy fine, or a year's imprisonment. The pattern of persecution which Mary Tudor had begun against the Protestants was now reversed, and under Elizabeth, the number of executions of Catholics for religious 'crimes' rose from two in 1583 to 34 in 1588.

Dissatisfied with portraits painted of herself to date, Elizabeth commissioned a Devon man, Nicholas Hilliard, who was England's leading miniaturist painter, to paint her likeness. Previously, in 1581, Hilliard had painted two portraits of Francis Drake, at his own request.

Meanwhile, Francis Drake was fortunate in that, for the remainder of his lifetime, he would have a sovereign, Queen Elizabeth, of the same Protestant persuasion as himself. Whether, in the testing times which were to come, Drake (whose constant companion was John Foxe's *Book of Martyrs*, a graphic account of the persecution of Protestants in the reign of Queen Mary I) would have fought so enthusiastically for a Catholic monarch as he did for Elizabeth, must be a matter for conjecture!

Drake Circumnavigates the Globe – From Plymouth to the Straits of Magellan

Francis Fletcher, preacher and pastor to Drake's ship, referring to Drake's astonishing feat of circumnavigating the earth, wrote 'that valiant enterprise, accompanied with happy success, which that rare and thrice worthy Captain Francis Drake achieved, in first turning up a furrow about the whole world, doth not only overmatch the ancient Argonauts, but also outreacheth, in many respects, that noble mariner Magellanus (Magellan) and by far surpasseth his crowned victory'.[1]

Born in 1480 to a noble family of Portugal, Ferdinand Magellan was anxious to travel to, and trade with, the Spice Islands (Moluccas, Indonesia). Unable to obtain sponsorship from his own King, he was granted funding from the teenage King Charles I of Spain, and duly gathered together a fleet of five ships and 270 men, which set sail in September, 1519.

The voyage was not a happy one, the Spanish sea captains resenting having a Portuguese in command. The result was that at Port St Julian in Patagonia (present day Argentina), Magellan was obliged to execute some of his men, who had been plotting to kill him and take command of the fleet.

In October, 1520 he discovered and sailed through the channel linking the Atlantic Ocean to the Pacific. This he named the 'Straits of All Saints'; it was later named after him the 'Straits of Magellan'. Because of the numerous Indian camp fires which they saw burning on shore at night time, they called this land 'Tierra del Fuego' (Land of Fire).

Magellan had no idea of the vastness of the Pacific Ocean, and his crossing of it took approximately four months. Having stopped at Guam, they reached the Philippines on March 28, 1521. It was here that Magellan was killed in a battle with the natives.

Only one ship of his fleet, the *Victoria*, completed the circumnavigation and returned safely to Spain. Of the remainder, one was shipwrecked, one deserted and returned the way it had come, one was abandoned, and one was captured by the Portuguese. The *Victoria* arrived home on

September 6, 1522, with 18 crew. She was the first vessel to have circumnavigated the globe.

So what were the circumstances which led to Drake following in Magellan's footsteps? He (Drake) was never one of Queen Elizabeth's suitors, yet she undoubtedly recognised his worth, as is evidenced by a document she gave to him which authorised him to attack enemy shipping, including that of Spain. Spanish Ambassador Mendoza was to say of him, 'The Queen shows extraordinary favour to Drake, and never fails to speak to him when she goes out in public, conversing with him for a long time'.[2]

At that time there was much interest in the possible existence of a navigable waterway around North America, linking the Atlantic and Pacific Oceans, the so-called north-west passage. Such a route would provide a short cut to the fabled Spice Islands of the East Indies, and avoid any clash with the Spaniards, whose colonies were further to the south. There was also speculation about the possible existence of 'Terra Incognita', a vast continent in the southern ocean; stretching southwards from South America and separated from it only by the Straits of Magellan. Here the English might find trade to rival that of the Portuguese in the east, or that of Spain in the 'New World'.

In 1573-4, a group of West Country adventurers, led by Cornish seaman Sir Richard Grenville, put forward a plan, the text of which still survives to this day – though some of the words are indecipherable – the document having been damaged by fire. The text mentions the South Sea and a latitude of 30', which is just to the north of the Chilean capital, Santiago. The words 'spices, drugs, cochineal' and 'special commodities' point to a proposed landing on the Chilean coast. Drake was then 'to return by the same way homewards as he went out'. The voyage, 'by God's favour', was to be completed in thirteen months, five of which were to be spent 'tarrying upon the coasts, to get knowledge of the princes and countries there'.[3] Clearly the aim was to befriend the inhabitants of the western coast of southern South America, and establish trading posts in areas not yet colonised by Spain.

To this end Drake and Thomas Doughty, whom he had met and befriended in Ireland and who was now private secretary to the lawyer and courtier Sir Christopher Hatton, came to London to seek the Queen's consent for such a voyage. The 'plan' mentioned the names of the Earl of Lincoln (Lord High Admiral of England); Sir William Winter

(Surveyor of the Navy and Master of Ordnance); his brother George Winter (Clerk to the Queen's ships); and John Hawkins (shortly to become Treasurer to the Navy). This indicates that the Navy Board supported the venture.

Of those close to the Queen, the Earl of Leicester (a privy councillor and one of her favourites), Sir Francis Walsingham (one of the principal Secretaries of State), and courtier Sir Christopher Hatton were in favour. However, Lord Burghley's (Lord Treasurer and Chief Advisor to the Queen) name was conspicuous by its absence. A shrewd and cautious man, he was anxious to avoid war with Spain. In the event the plan was approved; Drake being commanded by the Queen that, as regards the plan, the Lord Treasurer Burghley of all people, was not to know about it. Secrecy was also imperative if the Spaniards were not to discover Drake's intentions; and to this end false information was put out that he was to sail to the Mediterranean port of Alexandria, then part of the Turkish Empire, to open up a spice trade route.

The expenses of the voyage would be paid out of anticipated profits received from trade or plunder. Drake invested £1000 in the enterprise, Sir William Winter £750, and his brother George, and John Hawkins £500 apiece. Drake decided that Thomas Doughty and Doughty's brother John, would accompany him on the voyage. This was a decision which he would later come bitterly to regret.

Drake chose for his flagship the 120 ton, 18 gun *Pelican*, a ship with a remarkable history. One of many ships built and owned by William Bond (of the London family of merchant adventurers of that name), the *Pelican* had the misfortune to be taken by French pirates while sailing near Cherbourg. Her crew was killed, and her cargo valued at some £4000 captured. Subsequent efforts by William Bond to obtain redress by suing for damages were to no avail. By a strange coincidence, however, Francis Drake came across the ship (which was on her way back from Newfoundland with a cargo of fish) and captured her while he was sailing off Plymouth. He liked the *Pelican* so much that he refitted her and selected her for his present voyage, taking the trouble to include aboard her a forge for the making of nails and ironwork.[4]

The *Pelican* is described as being stout and strong, and 'a good sailer'. She had two 'sheathings' (i.e. a double-skinned hull, put in presumably at Drake's instigation), 'one (skin) as perfectly finished as the other'. She had 'seven armed portholes on each side', and carried 18 guns, 13 being of bronze and the remainder of cast iron.[5]

In company with the *Pelican* would sail the 80 ton, 16 gun *Elizabeth*, captained by George Winter's son John, as vice admiral, the 30 ton bark *Marigold*, the 50 ton flyboat (store-ship) *Swan*, the 15 ton pinnace *Christopher*, and the *Benedict*. Also present were Drake's brother Thomas, together with his fifteen-year-old cousin John who served as page (as he had done in the Irish campaign), and to whom fell the honour of dancing the hornpipe after Sunday Service. John Hawkins was not present. In 1559 or thereabouts, Hawkins had married Katharine, daughter of Benjamin Gonson, Treasurer of the Navy and, having previously been involved in naval administration, he now suceeded his father-in-law in the post. However, his nephew William also sailed with the fleet.

These ships Drake manned with 164 'able and sufficient men', wrote the chaplain, Francis Fletcher (who kept an account of the voyage) and 'furnished them also with such plentiful provision of all things necessary, as so long and dangerous a voyage did seem to require'. As well as Englishmen, they included Frenchmen, Danes, Flemings, Scotsmen, and even Biscayans. These vessels also carried a number of prefabricated pinnaces (a ship's small boat, either schooner-rigged or 8-oared), which were to be 'set up in smoother water, when occasion served'. Neither had Drake 'omitted to make provision also for ornament and delight', and to this end he carried with him 'expert musicians, rich furniture (all the vessels for his table, yea, many belonging even to the cook-room, being of pure silver), and divers shows of all sorts of curious workmanship, whereby the civility and magnificence of his native country might, amongst all nations whithersoever he should come, be the more admired'.

Drake's cabin, which was panelled in oak, contained a bed and a chair; also a desk on which he kept his charts, books and instruments. His sea-chest was bound in leather, and on the inside of its lid were paintings of the *Pelican*, as seen from various angles.

The fleet left Plymouth Sound on November 15, 1577, but was forced into Falmouth by adverse winds. There the ships were damaged by a storm, despite being in the shelter of the harbour, and the fleet was forced back to Plymouth to make repairs. On December 13, it put to sea once more and sailed for the Moroccan island of Mogador, whose Moorish kingdom was ruled by the King of Fez.

Despite being 'right courteously entertained with a dainty banquet', the Moors, suspicious of Drake's intentions, took one of his men, John Fry, a prisoner. The general (Drake), being 'grieved with this show of injury', put a company of men ashore but failed to locate their man. Fry was eventually released, only to find that the fleet had sailed. However, by the favour of the King, he was allowed to return home in an English merchant's ship.

Several more vessels were captured on the way to Cape Blanco on the Moroccan coast, which they reached on January 16, including three Spanish fishing boats ('canters'), and a caravel (light sailing ship). Having entered the harbour, they discovered that the place 'afforded plenty of fresh victuals, for the present refreshing of our men, and for their future supply at sea'.

During their six-day stay, some of the inhabitants of Cape Blanco visited Drake, bringing with them 'a woman, a Moor (with her little babe hanging upon her dry dug, having scarce life in herself, much less milk to nourish her child)'. Their intention was for the unfortunate woman to be sold 'as a horse, or a cow and calf by her side, in which sort of merchandise our general would not deal'. However, the inhabitants also brought 'amber-gris (a wax-like secretion of the intestine of the sperm whale, used in perfume manufacture), with certain gums (possibly gum arabic, obtained from some species of acacia and used as a glue and in incense) of some estimation', which they hoped to exchange for fresh water to quench their thirst. This water they took away in allforges (leathern bags for holding liquor). Drake, however, would 'receive nothing of them for water, but freely gave it (to) them that came to him, yea, and fed them... with our victuals'. Fletcher described their eating habits as 'not only uncivil and unsightly to us, but even inhuman and loathsome in itself'.

This good deed done, they released all the Spanish prizes except for one canter, for which they gave the owner the *Christopher* and one other vessel in exchange, and sailed for Mayo, one of the Cape Verde Islands, which was under the domain of the King of Portugal. By now Drake had made it clear that it was his intention to sail not for Alexandria, as previously stated, but across the Atlantic Ocean to Brazil.

At Mayo they found 'a great number of desolate and ruinous houses with a poor, naked chapel or oratory', but were shunned by the people who lived there, wrote Francis Fletcher. Here were to be had goats in plenty, and an 'infinite store of wild hens, and salt (to be obtained) without labour'.

West of Mayo was the island of Santiago, which was inhabited by both Portuguese and Moors together. This was because the Portuguese had exercised such 'extreme and unreasonable cruelty over their (Moorish) slaves that (their bondage being intolerable)', the slaves were forced to 'fly into the most mountainous parts of the island' where they now lived.

Here they took a 'Portugal' (Portuguese ship). She was bound for Brazil with a cargo of wine and cloth, with 'many gentlemen and merchants in her'. This ship, the *Santa Maria*, now joined the fleet and was renamed the *Mary*.

South-west of Santiago they discovered a volcanic island, which the Portuguese called 'Fuego' (the fiery furnace), within the bowels of which was 'a consuming fire, maintained by sulphury matters, seeming to be of a marvellous depth, and also very wide. The fire showeth itself but four times in an hour, at which times it breaketh out with such violence and force, and in such main abundance, that besides that it giveth light like the moon a great way off, it seemeth that it would not stay till it touch the heavens themselves'.

On the south side of the island was another island called Bravo (the brave island). Its only inhabitant was a hermit, who was 'so delighted in his solitary living, that he would by no means abide our coming, but fled, leaving behind him the relics of his false worship: to wit, a cross with a crucifix, and altar with his superaltar, and certain other idols of wood and rude workmanship'.

Here they released some of the Portuguese. It was very much in character for Drake to be mindful of welfare of his prisoners and to this end he gave the Portuguese (in exchange for their old ship), a pinnace, together with 'wine, bread and fish for their provision'. However, as Fletcher recorded, a member of their company chose not to be released, namely their pilot, 'a man well travelled both in Brazilia and most parts of India...' who, when he heard that they were en route to the 'Mare del Sur', (South Sea), expressed his willingness to go with them. This was Nuno da Silva, an experienced navigator whom Drake relieved of his astrolabe and navigation chart. However, this chart covered the Atlantic Ocean only as far as Rio de la Plata (the River Plate, between Uruguay and Argentina).[6]

On February 2, 1578 they set off on their voyage, in the course of which they sailed for sixty-three days 'without sight of land', and crossed the equator on the 17th. They had decided beforehand that in the event of them becoming separated, the appointed place of rendezvous would be the River Plate. In fact the journey was fraught and enervating, and during the course of it they often met with 'adverse winds, unwelcome storms', and 'less welcome calms... being as it were in the bosom of the burning zone', where they 'felt the effects of sultry heat'. This was in addition to 'the affrights of flashing lightnings, and terrifying claps of thunder...'. Fortunately, however, not one day passed but it rained, 'whereby our want of water was much supplied'.

The monotony of this voyage through the 'Doldrums' was only broken by the religious services, held twice a day and conducted principally, not by the chaplain, Francis Fletcher, but by Drake himself. A table and chairs were placed on the poop deck, and when he banged his hand twice on the table top, this was the signal for those men who were not on duty to take their place around it. Drake would then kneel on an embroidered cushion and read the psalms for the day, with the crew giving the responses.

Sundays were special days, when Drake and his officers and gentlemen wore their finest clothes, and the ship was dressed with flags. Chaplain Fletcher preached a sermon and at the end of the service, Drake's cousin John would dance a hornpipe. Again, showing characteristic thoughtfulness, Drake did not require his prisoners to be present at these services, for he realised that if this fact were to become known when they were released, then the utmost cruelties would await them at the hands of the Inquisition for such an 'offence' against the Catholic Church. However, prisoners or guests of rank or importance, such as Nuno da Silva, were often invited to join Drake and the gentlemen at the meal table as guests.

Fletcher was fascinated by the 'many strange creatures' which they saw, in particular a flying fish, 'of the bigness and proportion of a reasonable or middle sort of pilchard' with fins 'the length of his whole body... and supplying the like use to him that wings do to other creatures. By the help of these fins, when he is chased of (by) the bonito, or great mackerel' (who in turn is pursued by the aurata or dolphin), and 'hath not the strength to escape by swimming any longer' he therefore 'lifteth himself up above the water, and flieth a pretty height, sometimes lighting into boats or barks as they sail along'.

On April 5, they reached the coast of Brazil, where no suitable harbour could be found and a violent storm caused the *Christopher* to become separated from them. On April 14 they entered the River Plate as planned, and in a bay beneath another cape they found 'sweet and wholesome water'. Drake named it 'Cape Joy', for it was here that the *Christopher* was reunited with them.

Having anchored further up river, they killed some seals, (or 'sea wolves' as the Spaniards called them), which provided good meat, not only for the present but also for the future. Due to strong winds and shoals (areas of shallow water), they could only spend a fortnight here, and then, just as they reached the open sea again, the flyboat *Swan* became separated from them. This misfortune made Drake decide to reduce the number of his ships, so that those remaining might 'the better keep company'. In the meantime, in another storm, the captured Spanish fishing canter also became separated. On May 12, they sighted land and anchored; Drake named the place 'Cape Hope', because the bay with its headland provided an excellent harbour. Firstly, however, it had to be reconnoitred for rocks.

Fletcher described how Drake always displayed not only great courage, but an immense attention to detail, on occasions such as this. His 'general... was never wont to rely only on other men's care (judgment), how trusty or skilful soever they might seem to be; but always condemning danger, and refusing no toil, he was wont himself to be one... at every turn, where courage, skill, or industry was to be employed'. And nor would Drake 'entrust the discovery of these dangers to another's pains, but rather to his own experience in searching out and sounding of them'. Therefore, next morning when a small boat was launched it was Drake himself, in company with a few others, who set off for the shore, whereupon one of the natives appeared, 'seeming very pleasant, singing and dancing, after the noise of a rattle which he shook in his hand, expecting earnestly his landing'.

Thick fog and an extreme storm now forced them to run out to sea for their own safety. On May 14, however, the weather moderated and Drake went ashore and lit fires as a sign for the ships to reassemble again. However, both the *Mary* and the *Swan* failed to appear.

Meanwhile the inhabitants, 'for fear of our coming', had dispersed, but 'in houses made for that purpose', they found a 'great store of ostriches, at least to the number of 50, with much other fowl, some dried and some in drying for their provision...'. Fletcher, who had clearly never seen an ostrich before, wrote about it in some detail. Their 'thighs were in bigness equal to reasonable legs of mutton. They cannot fly at all; but they run so swiftly, and take so long strides, that it is not possible for a man in running by any means to take them, neither yet to come so nigh them as to have any shot at them either with bow or piece'. In order to 'betray' (mislead) these ostriches, the natives would place 'a great and large plume of feathers, orderly compact together upon the end of a staff, in the forepart bearing the likeness of the head, neck and bulk of an ostrich, and in the hinder part spreading itself out very large, sufficient to hide the most part of the body of a man'. With this they would stalk the birds, and drive them into 'some strait or neck of land close to the seaside, where spreading long and strong nets, with their dogs which they have in readiness at all times, they overthrow them, and make a common quarry'.

Continuing southward on May 15, they came to another bay where they anchored for fifteen days. From here, Drake sent Captain Winter southward, while he himself went northward, 'to see if happily they might meet with either of them (the *Swan* or the *Mary*)'. Drake did meet with the *Swan*, and brought her back to the harbour where, having unloaded her cargo, he deliberately cast her adrift. Her ironwork, however, was salvaged and her timbers kept for firewood and the making of implements.

Nearby was an island, the inhabitants of which made their appearance, 'leaping, dancing, and holding up their hands, and making outcries after their manner'. At this, Drake sent a boat, which contained 'such things as he thought would delight them', such as knives, bells and bugles. When the natives refused to come near, Drake's men tied these objects 'with a string upon a rod, and stuck the same up a reasonable distance from them, where they might see it'. Then, as soon as Drake's men had departed, the natives returned and removed the objects, leaving behind 'as in recompense, such feathers as they used to wear about their heads, with a bone made in the manner of a toothpick, carved round about the top, and in length about six inches, being very smoothly burnished'. Now Drake, 'with divers (several) of his gentlemen and company', went across to the mainland, where the natives, although fearful, presented him with presents of 'arrows of reeds, feathers, and such bones as are afore described'.

These people went about naked, observed Francis Fletcher, except for wearing 'a skin of fur, which they cast about their shoulders when they sit or lie in the cold'; however, when going about their work, they used the fur 'as a girdle about their loins'. Some washed their faces with sulphur, or some similar substance; others painted their whole bodies black, leaving only their necks white; and others still painted one shoulder black and the other white.

One of the chief natives, having been given one of Drake's own (head) caps, 'which he did daily wear', removed himself 'but a little from us', and 'with an arrow, pierced his leg deeply, causing the blood to stream out upon the ground: signifying thereby how unfeignedly he loved him (Drake), and giving therein a covenant of peace'. Edward Cliffe, however, who sailed with Winter in the *Elizabeth*, gives a different version of the 'cap' incident. The natives, he said, although much given to mirth and jollity, were very sly, and ready to steal anything that came within their reach, for one of them 'snatched our General's cap from his head (as he stooped) being of scarlet with a golden band (i.e. the cap)'. Nevertheless, Drake's sense of decency did not desert him, and despite this unfriendly act, he 'would suffer no man to hurt any of them'.[7]

Other islands they found to be so replete with birds and fowls that 'a wonderful multitude of people might be nourished' by them 'for many posterities'. Of these they killed 'some with shot and some with staves, and took some with our hands from men's heads and shoulders, upon which they lighted'. This they named 'Seal Bay', by reason of the plentiful number of seals thereabouts.

On June 3 they set sail southwards once more, 'towards the pole Antarctic', until they came across a little bay in which they anchored for two days. Here, in accordance with Drake's philosophy of reducing the size of the fleet, they abandoned the *Christopher*.

When they were within one degree of the mouth of the Straits of Magellan, which they knew would provide their passage into the 'South Sea' (Pacific), Drake altered course, hoping that 'happily God would grant we might find our ship (*Mary*) and friends whom we lost in the great storm...'.

On June 19 they found the *Mary*, for which they 'gave God thanks with most joyful minds'. However the ship, 'by reason of extremity of weather which she had endured', was in such a poor state that Drake decided to put into Port St Julian with his fleet, 'there to refresh his wearied men'.

Having come to anchor, Drake in company with his brothers Thomas and John, Robert Winter, Oliver the master gunner, John Brewer and Thomas Hood, went ashore to seek provisions. As ever, Drake led by example, and in Fletcher's words, 'did not... think himself discharged of his duty if he himself bestowed not the first travail therein'.

Having landed, he was approached by two of the inhabitants of that place, to whom Magellan had given the name 'Pentagours', 'from their huge stature and strength proportionable'. At first the Pentagours seemed pleased to see them and took great pleasure in watching Oliver shoot an arrow; attempting to do the same themselves, they achieved nothing like the same distance! However, treachery was afoot, because as Drake and his company went 'quietly without any suspicion of evil' towards their boat, the natives, having stealthily crept up behind them, shot at them with arrows. One pierced the lungs of Robert Winter, who had also been demonstrating with the bow, 'yet he fell not', and Oliver the master gunner, whose caliver (light musket) had failed to discharge itself, 'was presently slain outright'. Now Drake's bravery saved the day, for in Fletcher's words, had he (Drake) not 'valiantly thrust himself into the dance against these monsters, then none of the men who had landed would have escaped with his life'.

Drake took the caliver 'which the gunner could not make to take fire', and thereby 'dispatched the first beginner of the quarrel, the same man which slew our master gunner'. This weapon, 'being charged with a bullet, and hail shot (small shot that scatters like hail), and well aimed, tore out his belly and guts, with great torment, as it seemed by his cry, which was so hideous and horrible a roar, as if ten bulls had been joined together in roaring'. At this the natives, who had apparently not realised that 'our calivers (light muskets), swords and targets (shields) were any munition or weapon of war', turned tail and fled.

Drake now chose to depart but again, maintaining his dignity and composure, he abstained from taking revenge on the natives, something which he could so easily have done. As for the wounded man, Robert Winter, 'whom for (his) many good parts he (Drake) loved dearly', he died the day after he was brought back aboard the ship.

The bodies of Oliver and Winter were laid to rest in a single grave, 'with such reverence as was fit for the earthen tabernacle of immortal souls, and with such commendable ceremonies as belong to soldiers of worth in time of war, which they most truly and rightfully deserved'. The fleet then departed.

Fletcher's view, presumably shared by Drake, was that the 'Spanish cruelties' inflicted on the Pentagours, so-called because the 'highest of them' measured five cubits (7½ feet), 'had made them the more inhospitable to … any strangers that shall come hereafter.'

⌒

As for Thomas Doughty, supposedly a friend of Drake, Fletcher described his qualities in glowing terms; 'a sweet orator' and 'philosopher', with 'a good gift for the Greek tongue and a reasonable taste of Hebrew'. Also, 'a sufficient secretary to a noble personage of great place, and in Ireland, an approved soldier, and not behind many in the study of the law for his time...'.

According to Fletcher, 'to this evil, thus received at the hands of infidels (the Pentagours), there was adjoined and grew another mischief, wrought and contrived closely amongst ourselves', and with 'far more grievous consequences than the former'. Doughty was proving to be a mischief-maker par excellence!

Loyalty was a quality greatly esteemed by Drake, and at first he could not believe that 'a person whom he loved so dearly' was capable of such plots (whatever they may have been, for this is not made clear). Therefore not only did he 'continue all countenance, credit and courtesies, which he was wont to show and give him (Doughty), but increased them'. In fact not long after, Drake appointed Doughty captain of the *Mary*.

Doughty was now accused by members of the *Mary's* company of having 'purloined to his private use... some things of great value...'. Drake lost no time in going aboard to investigate the matter, and found only 'certain pairs of Portuguese gloves, some few pieces of money of a strange coin, and a small ring', all of which, said Doughty, 'one of the Portugals (Portuguese prisoners) gave him out of his chest in hope of favour', and which were 'not worth the speaking of'. Doughty having thus been apparently vindicated, Drake now appointed him commander of his own flagship, the *Pelican*, whilst he transferred to the *Mary*. Some remaining Portuguese prisoners were provided with a pinnace and victuals and released.

Aboard the *Pelican*, Doughty proved to be equally unpopular, and was accused of being 'too peremptory', and of exceeding his authority. An exasperated Drake now returned to his flagship, and 'removed the said Doughty prisoner into the fly boat with utter disgrace'.

Forty of the most senior men in the fleet were now appointed to try Thomas Doughty, on a charge of mutiny and witchcraft. It was probably no coincidence that Drake chose for the trial a small island at Port St Julian, which they reached on June 30, 1578; for it was here that Ferdinand Magellan had executed mutineers from his own ship in 1520. In fact, here on the mainland, Drake's men 'found a gibbet, fallen down, made of a spruce (ship's) mast, with men's bones underneath it...'; presumably a legacy of that voyage.

Drake told the jury that the Queen had expressly forbidden the true purpose of his expedition to be revealed to anyone, and especially not to Lord Treasurer Burghley, who wished to postpone any war with Spain until England was stronger. To this, Doughty coolly replied that he had already told Burghley 'the plot of the voyage'. This admission by Doughty sealed his fate, and a verdict of 'guilty' was returned. Drake then gave Doughty the choice of either being executed on the island, or left on land, or to return to England, 'there to answer for his deed before the Lords of Her Majesty's Council'. Of the three, Doughty chose the first.

With preacher Fletcher presiding, Drake and Doughty took Holy Communion together, after which they dined at the same table, 'as cheerfully in sobriety as ever in their lives they had done aforetime; each cheering up the other, and taking their leave by drinking to each other, as if some journey only had been in hand'. Even in such extremity, the niceties had to be observed. Then without any further delay, Doughty came forward, knelt down, and prepared 'his neck for the axe, and his spirit for heaven...'. He was buried on the island, which was now named 'the island of true justice and judgment'.

John Cooke was a sailor aboard *Elizabeth*. His account is less flattering to Drake than that of Fletcher.[8] According to Cooke, having taken 'a good store of drink' from the Portuguese prize (captured off the Island of Santiago), Drake entrusted it to the custodianship of Thomas Doughty. However, Drake's brother, Thomas, ignoring Drake's instructions, broke open one of the chests, whereupon Doughty remonstrated with him. Thomas Drake then admitted his mistake, and asked Doughty to keep his misdemeanour a secret. Doughty refused, but when he broached the matter, Drake flew into a rage, and enquired what

Doughty 'should mean to touch (impugn) his brother'. This, said Cooke, was the source of all the future grievances between Drake and Doughty; from then on, Drake 'daily sought matter against Master Doughty, seeking at every man's hands what they could inveigh against him'.

Doughty was not permitted to speak to Drake, who struck him, had him tied to the mast, and described him as a 'conjurer and witch', a 'seditious' and a 'very bad and lewd fellow', a poisoner, and the 'occasioner (cause)' of any foul weather which they happened to encounter. Doughty's woes 'did daily increase through this tyrannical government...'.

At the Port of St Julian, Drake 'spewed out' against Doughty, 'all his venom' and 'conceived hatred'. When, at his trial, Doughty asked to see the commission by which he was charged, Drake refused. One of the charges was that Doughty had allegedly told Edward Bright (ship's carpenter aboard the *Marigold*), that 'the Queen's majesty and counsel would be corrupted'. This Doughty denied.

There was another twist in the tail. Doughty had apparently, when drunk, 'blabbed out' to Drake that he 'lived intimately' with Drake's wife, Mary.[9] If this were the case, it would explain Drake's seeming hatred of Doughty.

掗掗

To silence any further dissent, Drake beat his drum to summon every man ashore. Then flanked by Captain Thomas of the *Marigold* on the one side, and by Captain Wynter of the *Elizabeth* on the other, he made a speech in which he told his men what he expected of them. 'The mutinies and discords that are grown amongst us,' he said, 'doth even take my wits from me to think on it...' and the 'stomaching between the gentlemen and sailors... doth even make me mad to hear it. But, my masters, I must have it left, for I must have the gentleman to hale (haul) and draw with the mariner, and the mariner with the gentleman... I would know him that would refuse to set his hand to a rope, but I know there is not any such here,' he said, tempering sternness with a desire to think the best of his men. If any men's hearts failed them, then he, Drake, would allot a ship for their passage home. 'You come then of your own will: on you it depends to make the voyage renowned...'. If they gave up now it would be 'a reproach to our country' and they would make themselves 'a laughing-stock to the enemy'. To their astonishment, Drake then formally relieved all the officers (with the exception of those aboard the *Marigold*), who in the main had been appointed by the ship-owners, of their commands; only to reinstate them immediately as his own appointees. By this action, he strengthened his control, whilst at the same time making it clear that all were equally involved in the venture, despite the distinction of class or rank. If it succeeded, they would all be rich men![10]

At Port St. Julian they disposed of the *Mary* 'because she was leak and troublesome'. Her skeleton was left on the beach where, for the previous two months of rest and repair, they had pitched their tents. Then on August 17, having tarred the hulls of their remaining three ships, *Pelican*, *Elizabeth* and *Marigold*, from top to bottom, they set sail once more.

Did Drake know where the Straits of Magellan were? The answer is undoubtedly, yes. It is known for certain that he carried with him a copy made by Abraham Ortelius of Antwerp in 1570 (who in 1573 was appointed cosmographer to Philip II of Spain) of a map of the world produced by Gerhardus Mercator (Flemish geographer and map-maker). Drake was also able to benefit from other maps belonging to Nuno da Silva, pilot of the captured ship *Santa Maria*.[11]

Near the entrance to the Straits of Magellan was a cape (which the Spaniards called Capo Virgin Maria), where 'in homage to our sovereign lady the Queen's Majesty', Drake commanded the ships 'to strike their topsails upon the bunt (furl their sails) as a token of his willing and glad mind, to show his dutiful obedience to her Highness'. Here also, 'in remembrance of his honourable friend (and sponsor), Sir Christopher Hatton', he changed the name of the *Pelican* to *Golden Hind*, the name of the antelope that appeared on Hatton's crest.

John Drake, his artistic nephew, was then instructed to embellish the *Golden Hind* with Hatton's coat of arms, and to paint the stern of the vessel in the red and yellow of his livery; whilst the ship's carpenter made a figurehead of a hind to replace that of the pelican.

Even at this early stage of the voyage, Drake was beginning to live up to his motto – *Sic Parvis Magna* – which appeared on his own coat of arms, on the cannons of his ship, on his furniture aboard, and on his famous captain's drum.

6

The Circumnavigation – From the Straits to 'New Albion'

Having entered the Straits of Magellan on August 24, 1578 they came across three islands, the largest of which Drake landed upon and took possession of, for the Queen, naming it 'Elizabeth Island'. The other two he named Bartholomew, 'according to the day' (it was St Bartholomew's Day); and Saint George's, 'in honour of England'.

The land on both sides was high and mountainous. On the one side lay the continent of South America, and on the other, nothing but islands; with 'innumerable frets' (passages) into the Pacific. There were also many 'shuttings up', where there was no passage at all. Contrary winds were 'a great hindrance', but nevertheless, what Magellan had taken thirty-seven days to negotiate, Drake accomplished in only sixteen. When news of Drake's passage through the Straits of Magellan reached King Philip of Spain he was furious, since he considered the Straits to be his own property.

The following day they encountered a storm so extreme that it appeared to them as if God 'had pronounced a sentence, not to stay His hand, nor to withdraw His judgment, till he had buried our bodies, and ships also, in the bottomless depth of the raging sea'. These 'violent and extraordinary flaws (such as seldom have been seen), continued into the night, and caused the *Marigold*, in which was Captain John Thomas, with many other of our dear friends...' to become separated. In this event, the possibility of which Drake had foreseen, the appointed place of rendezvous was to be at latitude

Drake's chest, from his cabin on the Golden Hind.

Photo: Berkeley Castle, Gloucestershire.

30 degrees, on the coast of Peru.

This storm continued for a whole month, until at nightfall on October 7, the two remaining ships entered a harbour which they had previously noticed on leaving the Straits, this after being driven southwards to a latitude of 57 degrees. However, within a few hours, the 'violence and fury of the flaw (wind)' caused Drake to lose an anchor, and also the company of his vice admiral, the *Elizabeth* with her complement of 50 men. In fact, there was a strong element on the *Elizabeth* who were anxious to leave all these troubles behind; and the ship, having re-entered the Straits the next day, set sail for home and arrived in Plymouth on June 2 of the following year, 1579.

Meanwhile, having set sail again, the *Golden Hind* was once more driven southwards, this time to latitude 55 degrees. Here they came across some islands where they enjoyed 'some quietness for a very little time'. The men were weak, and in poor health, but here they found fresh water and 'divers good and wholesome herbs' which afforded great help and refreshing to our weak and sickly bodies'.

Again, the winds returned, making the sea rage, and blowing 'such as if all the clouds under heaven had been called together to lay their force upon that one place'. The 'tempest' had now lasted a full fifty-two days.

They sailed southwards and again anchored in amongst some islands, to which Drake gave the collective name, the 'Elizabethides', but after a three-day breathing space the storms returned; this time blowing the ship to 'the uttermost part of land towards the South Pole'. Fletcher's statement that the 'uttermost cape of all these islands stands near in 56 degrees', indicates that they had discovered Cape Horn, and that there was no land mass to the southwards. The fabled 'Terra Incognita', 'wherein many strange monsters lived' did not therefore exist. The storms ended on October 28, Fletcher observing that night time, at that time of year, lasted for a mere two hours. Two days later they sailed northwards. Up until now, 30 or more men had been lost, not only in skirmishes with local Indians, but also from cold and from malnutrition. Whether it ever entered Drake's mind to attempt to return home is not known, but he did know that were he to do so, then the Spaniards would be waiting for him.

They found the coast of what they thought was Peru (but which was in fact Chile) to be 'mountainous and barren, without water or wood', and for the most part 'inhabited by the Spaniards and few others'. At 37 degrees, there being no news of the other two ships (unbeknown to them, the *Marigold*, whose captain John Thomas had been a most valuable asset as he could speak fluent Spanish, with crew of 29, had been lost with all hands), they anchored at the island of Mocha. This was a 'fruitful place... well stored with sundry sorts of good things', such as sheep, cattle, maize and potatoes. Its Indian inhabitants had fled here from the Main, owing to the 'cruel and most extreme dealing of the Spaniards'.

The Indians appeared to be pleased to see them, and promised to bring fresh water early the next morning. Drake set off accordingly in the ship's boat, with a party of 11 bowmen and harquebusiers, but he was cautious in that he allowed only two men to go ashore with barricoes (casks) to the assigned watering place. Here, instead of being welcomed, the two were immediately 'set upon by those traitorous people', 500 or so well-armed men who had lain behind the rocks in ambush, and 'suddenly slain'. Drake was 'shot in the face, under his right eye, and close by his nose', and the other nine people in the boat were all wounded. Moreover, there was no surgeon in attendance; the chief one being dead, and the other being absent in the missing *Elizabeth*. Drake had a rudimentary knowledge of surgery and, despite his own wounds, was able to give assistance to his men, all of whom recovered.

Again, the hostile behaviour of the natives was attributed to 'the deadly hatred which they bear against their cruel enemies, the Spaniards', for whom they had mistaken Drake and his men. Drake, who had sufficient insight to realise this, chose once again not to revenge this wrong, but instead committed the Indians to God, 'wishing this only punishment to them', for they were not aware that they had done 'this injury, not to an enemy, but to a friend; not to a Spaniard, but to an Englishman...'.

They now turned southwards, and on November 30 reached a bay called Philips Bay, where an Indian approached the *Golden Hind* in a canoe. 'Partly by signs, and partly by (showing him) such things as we had', Drake's men indicated what they required and he and his 'captain' returned accordingly with 'some hens, eggs, a fat hog, and such like'. Their captain also offered to pilot them to a good harbour not far to the southward.

The Spaniards called this harbour Valparaiso, and the town which adjoined it, Saint James of Chile ('Santiago', Chile's capital city), where they found 'divers storehouses of the wines of Chile'. In the harbour was a ship called *La Capitana*, admiral to the Islands of Solomon (discovered by the Spaniards in 1567), in which they found wines, a quantity of fine gold from the mines of Valdivia, and 'a great cross of gold beset with emeralds, on which was nailed a god of the same metal'. As Fletcher says euphemistically, they eased this ship of its heavy burden, and refreshed themselves (doubtless with the wine!).

On December 8, having stocked up with wine, bread, bacon, etc, they set sail towards the equator. The Indian captain who acted as pilot was 'bountifully rewarded and enriched with many good things', by Drake, which 'pleased him exceedingly'. The pilot was then 'landed in the place where he desired'.

From prisoners Drake learned of his friend and former shipmate, John Oxenham. In 1575, Oxenham had fitted out a 120 ton ship with a crew of 70 for an expedition to the Isthmus of Panama. Having hidden his ship and built a pinnace in which he sailed down a river which led into the Pacific, he had hoped to intercept Spanish treasure ships en route from Peru to Panama. Oxenham and his men however, were intercepted by the Spaniards. All his crew members were either killed in skirmishes or executed, with the exception of himself, the master, the pilot and five ship's boys who were captured.

In a bay adjacent to the town of La Herradura, 14 of Drake's men were landed to seek out a likely place to stop off. However, they were immediately discovered by the Spaniards, of whom there were 100 mounted on horses; there were also 200 Indian slaves, who ran 'as dogs at their heels, all naked, and in most miserable bondage'. All escaped except for a Richard Minivy who was killed and then beheaded by the Spaniards. His right hand was cut off and his heart 'plucked out'. As for 'the rest of his carcass', they (the Spaniards) 'caused the Indians to shoot it full of arrows', after which it was left 'to be devoured of the beasts and fowls'.

On December 20 they reached another harbour where they spent time trimming the ship and building the pinnace. 'But still, grief for the absence of our friends remained with us,' said Fletcher, and in an attempt to locate the two lost ships, Drake and some chosen men took the pinnace and sailed southward for a day, only to be driven back by adverse winds.

Setting forth again and finding no adequate supply of fresh water on the island of Mormorena, they landed at Tarapaca (Colombia) where they discovered a Spaniard, lying asleep beside 13 bars of silver (to the value of about 4000 Spanish ducats). The Spaniard was woken up and 'freed of his charge'; Fletcher, with his dry sense of humour observing that, having been relieved of the responsibility of looking after his silver, the unfortunate man might now be able to sleep more soundly!

Fish of various kinds and sheep were exchanged for knives, margarites (trade name for pale, dry sherry-wine) and glasses (possibly drinking vessels). Fletcher noted that the sheep were of great size and strength. Three grown and tall men, and one boy could sit comfortably on their back, with 'no man's foot touching the ground by a large foot in length; the beast nothing at all complaining of his burden in the meantime'.

At Arica, where they arrived on February 7, 1579, they found a 'most pleasant and fertile valley'. Ships from this port sailed to and from Callao, the port for Lima, Peru's capital city. Here they relieved two barks of 'some forty odd bars of silver, of the bigness and fashion of a brick bat, and in weight each of them about 20 pounds'. En route to Lima, they impressed another bark into the fleet, as they thought its cargo of linen might stand them in good stead.

Despite the fact that the Spaniards had no less than 30 ships in Lima harbour, they boldly entered and 'anchored all night in the midst of them'. However, although in a position to 'make spoil amongst them', Drake and his men were more anxious to join up again with their two missing ships, rather than to seek retribution from the Spaniards for their 'cruel and hard dealing'.

At Callao, they plundered a ship belonging to one Miguel Angel, loaded with 1500 bars of gold plate. It was here that they learned of the death of three kings viz. those of Portugal, Morocco and Fez (a kingdom of Morocco), and more importantly to them, that a ship laden with gold and silver had sailed thirteen days earlier, bound for Panama.

When Drake learned that John Oxenham and seven of his ship's crew were currently languishing in prison at nearby Lima, he was grieved at his inability, through lack of sufficient resources, to mount a rescue attempt. All he could do was write to the Viceroy, threatening terrible reprisals, unless the Inquisition spared the lives of Oxenham and his men.

The following day, they set off in pursuit, crossing 'the line' (equator) on February 28. At Paita they captured a vessel owned and commanded by Bernito Diaz Bravo containing gold, silver, victuals and ships' tackle. It was alleged that Bravo's clerk, one Francisco Jacome, had witheld some treasure, so in order to make him talk, Drake had a rope placed around his neck. Jacome was momentarily hoisted from the deck before being allowed to fall into the sea from which he was rescued by the *Golden Hind's* boat. For Drake, the acquisition of treasure was a serious business, and he could be ruthless, when the occasion demanded. So anxious was Drake to capture the 'rich ship' that he offered a gold chain to whomsoever was first to sight her. In the event this was to be his nephew, John Drake, who was in the crow's nest and sighted her at midday on March 1, off Cape Francisco (Ecuador). By towing cables and wine jars astern of the *Golden Hind*, whilst at the same time leaving her sails unfurled, Drake misled his prey into thinking that he had not the speed to overtake. However, as night fell, the cables were cut and the *Golden Hind* quickly came alongside, removed the enemy ship's mizzen mast with a cannonball, and forced her to strike her sails (surrender).

The *Nuestra Senora De La Concepcion*, commonly known as the *Cacafuego* (literally 'Spitfire'), was captained by a Juan de Anton, and in her they found 'conserves, sugars, meal and other victuals'. Of great interest were 'a certain quantity of jewels and precious stones, 13 chests of rials ('royals') of plate (made of silver or gold and belonging to the King), 80 pound weight in gold, 26 ton of uncoined silver, two very fair gilt silver drinking bowls... valued in all at about 360,000 pesos'. 'Freeing him of the care with which his ship was loaden', they gave her master, in exchange for 'these commodities', 'a little linen and the like'.

Drake told de Anton that he had a commission from the Queen to commit robberies for her, and that all that he should acquire over and above the 7000 ducats that he claimed to have lost, in the ill-fated Hawkins expedition of 1568, he would give to Her Majesty. He also told de Anton of his concern for John Oxenham and the other English prisoners. 'Tell the Viceroy of Peru not to hang them' he said 'for if he does I swear it will cost the heads of 3000 men of Peru, all of which heads I will cast into the port of Callao'.[1] Drake's message did in fact reach the Viceroy, but only had the effect of prolonging the lives of the English prisoners until the following year, for as soon as Drake left American waters, Oxenham and his companions were executed. De Anton stated that 'the Englishman (Drake) was much feared by his men, and that he had people for a guard...'.[2]

It had taken six days to unload the *Cacafuego*, after which Drake released her captain de Anton and her crew unharmed, having exchanged courtesies and gifts, and provided him with credentials to give to Captain Wynter of the *Elizabeth*, should the two ever meet.

Drake continued northwards with his fleet; now numbering three ships, and the pinnace which scoured the inlets for likely prey. The fact that the Spaniards believed that they controlled these waters gave Drake an advantage. They did not anticipate any attack, and therefore none of their ships was armed.

Off the coast of Nicaragua, Drake captured a ship belonging to a Panamanian called Rodrigo Tello, whose crew he released with the exception of her pilot, one Alonso Sanchez Colchero, a native of Seville. Colchero was 'pilot of the Armada of the China route', in other words, Spain's trade route to the Philippines. Realising that this man might be useful to him, Drake tried to bribe him into cooperating; but this failed and Colchero was released. Colchero later claimed that Drake had terrified him by having him half-strangled, though this was never corroborated, and Colchero may simply have been repeating the experience of Francisco Jacome. Drake did however, take Colchero's 'sea cards' (charts) for future reference. The *Golden Hind's* treasure was then temporarily transferred to this ship while she was 'careened', that is, turned onto her side on a sandbank in order that her hull might be cleaned, re-caulked, and then greased with sulphur and tar.

They passed the El Salvadorian port of Sonsonate, where the volcanoes of Honduras and Guatemala came into view, rising up to 13,600 feet above sea level. Here, on April 4, Drake captured the Spanish merchantman *Espirito Santo*, commanded by Don Francisco de Zarate, the appellation 'Don' being reserved strictly for a person of quality or noble birth. In fact, Zarate was a cousin of the Duke of Medina Sidonia, with whom Drake would later come into conflict on a much larger stage. Drake treated Zarate with great courtesy, giving him his own cabin in the poop to sleep in, and allowing him to keep his rich clothing and Cross of the Order of St James, the emblem of military valour. In return, Zarate gave Drake a 'falcon of gold, handsomely wrought, with a great emerald set in the breast of it'. As they dined together, Drake helped Zarate to food, and told him not to worry as his life and property were safe, at which Zarate kissed Drake's hand.[3]

The treachery which Drake had encountered at San Juan de Ulua back in 1567 at the hands of Don Martin Enriquez, the Viceroy who had betrayed John Hawkins and himself, still rankled deeply within Drake's breast, and he therefore asked Zarate whether he knew Enriquez. The answer was yes, to which Drake replied, 'I would be more pleased to fall in with him than all the silver and gold in the Indies, and you would see how to comply with the word of a gentleman.'[4]

Zarate described Drake as 'one of the greatest mariners that sails the seas, both as a navigator and as a commander'. Drake, he said, was also careful to observe the niceties, for he 'dined and supped to the music of vigolones (probably bass-viols or violas)'. As for the protocol which Drake insisted must be observed aboard *Golden Hind*, Zarate commented as follows. 'He treats them (his men) with kindness and they treat him with respect. He has with him nine or ten gentlemen, second sons of some of the principal men in England. Some of these belong to his council, and he calls them together for any matter, no matter how simple it may be, although he takes orders from no one, but takes pleasure in hearing them, and having done so gives his orders. He has no favourite. These (gentlemen) he seats at his table, and even the Portuguese pilot (Nuno da Silva)... who did not speak a word during all the time I was on board. He (Drake) is served with much plate with his arms on it, which has the borders and the decorations gilded. He carries with him all the presents (presumably to be bestowed on deserving recipients during the voyage) and scented water possible, much of which he said had been given him by the Queen. None of these gentlemen sit down or cover themselves in front of him unless they are first ordered to do so, not only once, but many times.'[5]

As for the *Golden Hind* itself, she was 'a perfct sailer'. In addition to her 30 large guns, ammunition, and other 'necessary warlike stores', she carried a great quantity of 'engines for throwing fire'. She was a new vessel, with 'double sides' (i.e. a double-skinned hull), and carpenters and caulkers were carried so that the ship could be careened at any time. Her crew were as well-disciplined as the 'old Italian soldiers', and everyone took great care to keep his harquebus (portable gun with forked rest) clean.

'I understand that the crew are under (in receipt of) wages,' said Zarate, 'because in the sack of our ship, no one dared to take anything except as he ordered. He grants them (the men) many favours, and punishes them for the least fault.' Drake also had with him painters (artists), 'who paint the coast in its proper colours'. Everything was depicted so naturally, that 'whoever follows him could in no way lose himself'. Nuno da Silva confirms that Drake and his young cousin John were also adept at painting, at which they sat together for long hours in Drake's cabin. Drake also 'delineated birds, trees and sealions', in a book in which he also 'entered his navigation'.[6]

After three days, Zarate was released, but not before the customary exchanges of (further) gifts had taken place, or to be more correct, Drake helped himself to some little metal objects (unspecified, but probably ornaments), which he said were for his wife, in exchange for which he gave Zarate a cutlass and a little firepan (brazier) of silver.

An anonymous writer described how Drake removed from the *Espirito Santo* 'a pilot to carry him to the haven of Guatulco, and also a proper negro wench called Maria'. This person was clearly used as a prostitute, whether voluntary or involuntary is not recorded, because she was 'afterwards gotten with child between the captain and his men pirates'.[7]

This pilot, one Juan Pascual, Drake kept 'sometimes in iron and sometimes unfettered', to show him where to find water. Pascual, who was released at Guatulco, described how twice a day, before the lunchtime and the evening meal, Drake made his devotions. A table was produced, 'without a cloth or table cover'. Then Drake 'took out a very large book and knelt down, bareheaded, and read from the said book in his English language. All the other Englishmen... were also seated without their hats, and made responses. Some of them held books resembling Bibles in their hands and read in these... sometimes one of the Englishmen, whom all appeared to respect (this presumably was Fletcher), preached to them in the English tongue, and was listened to attentively'.

Drake realised that, having searched diligently and made careful enquiry in every harbour or creek that they came across, there was little hope of them coming across the missing ships. Now he would devote himself to the search for a passage around the northern parts of America, 'from the South Sea (Pacific), into our own Ocean (the Atlantic)'. This was the so-called Straits of Anian, depicted on Ortelius's World Map of 1564, and named after the Island of Anan, described by Marco Polo in his 'Travels'. Once discovered and found to be navigable, knowledge of this passage would not only be of benefit to his country, but would also provide them with a short cut home to England. Drake's men 'wilingly hearkened' to this proposal.

On the way to Cano, off Costa Rica, they 'unburdened' a vessel of its cargo of 'linen, China silk and China dishes' and 'a falcon of gold, handsomely wrought, with a great emerald set in the breast of it'. Here they experienced a severe earthquake, the force of which made their ship, and the pinnace which was sailing with her a mile off shore, shake and 'quiver as if it had been laid on dry land'. Here they found fish, fresh water, and wood, and saw 'alargartoes (alligators), and monkeys and the like...'.

At Guatulco, they were able to obtain from the Spaniards, 'many things which we desired, and chiefly bread...'. Now Drake released Nuno da Silva, captain of the captured Portuguese ship *Santa Maria*, who had been his prisoner and acting-pilot for the past fourteen months, along with other prisoners. Drake would surely have acted otherwise had he known that da Silva would be handed over to the Mexican Inquisition, suffer the fate of being tortured on the rack on suspicion of having turned heretic, and then languish in prison for four years before being released on the personal orders of King Philip.

Drake, unlike his Spanish foes and even some of his countrymen back in England, was not in the business of torturing people and putting them to death for their faith. Nevertheless, the contempt with which Drake and his men viewed the Catholic Church is revealed by the Spaniard Francisco Rengifo, Factor (agent) of the port of Guatulco. They robbed the church of its silver vessels, rich vestments and hangings, he said, and of 'five pairs of altar-cloths, which the Englishmen carried on their shoulders, using them to wipe the perspiration from their faces. Also a missal... and the box in which the unconsecrated wafers were kept, from which they took all the wafers and broke them into pieces and stamped them underfoot... they smashed the image of Our Lady, with Our Father and the Holy Ghost'. Rengifo's own home was robbed of everything it contained, including silver, gold and clothing to the value of about 7000 pesos in reals. The sacred images at the head of his bed and on his writing table were also broken to pieces. Rengifo reported that the boatswain of Drake's ship took a crucifix and struck it against a table, breaking it to pieces, saying to those Spaniards who witnessed the event, 'You ought indeed to be grieved for you are not Christians, but idolators who adore sticks and stones.'[8]

Between April 16 and June 3, 1579, they travelled a total of 1400 leagues (4200 nautical miles), up to a latitude of 42 degrees, where the men 'did grievously complain' of the 'pinching and biting air', where the rain fell as 'an unnatural, congealed and frozen substance'. The seamen were so cold that they hardly dared risk removing their hands from the warmth of their 'coverts' (pockets) to feed themselves, for fear of the 'cold that did benumb them'. The result was that before long, what three men had previously been able to perform, now '6 men, with their best strength and uttermost endeavour, were hardly able to accomplish'. Yet Drake was not to be discouraged, and 'by comfortable speeches' which mentioned 'the divine providence', and 'God's loving care over his children', he 'stirred them up to put on good courage'.

On June 5 they were forced by adverse winds to anchor in a 'bad bay'. The 'extremity of the cold' now forced them to journey south, from a latitude of 48 degrees. As they hugged the coast, they noticed that every hill was covered in snow, despite the time of year. Why had they journeyed so far northwards, despite the atrocious conditions? The most likely explanation is given by Thomas Blundeville, who in 1594, wrote several treatises on the art of navigation. 'Sir Francis himselfe (as I have heard)' he states 'was of a very good will to have sailed still more Northward, hoping to find passage through the narrow sea Anian.' In other words, Drake was looking for the fabled 'Northwest Passage' (sea route around the North American continent). Had he found it, it would have afforded him a quicker route back to England, free from Spanish interference.⁹

On June 17 they found a suitable bay in which to anchor, at a latitude of 38 degrees, 30 minutes. By now they had reluctantly come to the conclusion that the so-called Northwest Passage either did not exist, or if it did, that it was unnavigable. In fact the Northwest Passage did exist, but would not be negotiated by a European for another three centuries.

Three times, one of the native inhabitants approached in a canoe; on the third occasion bringing with him 'a bunch of feathers, much like the feathers of a black crow, very neatly and artificially gathered upon a string, and drawn together in a round bundle'. They learned later that those that guarded the king wore such an item as a headdress.

Four days later, all the men from the *Golden Hind* were landed and ordered to erect tents and make a fort, while a leak she had sustained at sea was repaired. The natives were entirely submissive, and 'nothing could remove that opinion which they had conceived of us, that we should be (i.e. were) gods'. In return for shirts, linen and cloth, they gave 'feathers, cauls of network (hair coverings), the quivers of their arrows (made of fawn skins), and the very skins of beasts that the women wore upon their bodies'.

The native men for the most part went about naked, whereas the women wore loose-fitting garments made from combed bullrushes which 'being knit (tightly worn) about their middles', hung down about their hips, and so afforded them 'a covering of that which nature teaches should be hidden'. Around their shoulders they wore 'the skin of a deer, with the hair upon it'.

Finally, their king arrived, 'a man of a goodly stature and comely personage, attended with his guard of about 100 tall and warlike men'. They seated Drake and, after 'orations' from the king and others, 'set the crown upon his head'. Now it was obvious that 'the chief god (that is, Drake) was now become their god, their king and patron, and themselves were become the only happy and blessed people in the world'.

Drake, anxious not to cause offence, accepted their offer by taking 'the sceptre, crown and dignity of the said country into his hand', on behalf of Her Majesty Queen Elizabeth.

On a journey inland, they saw a vast herd of 'very large and fat deer', and 'a multitude of a strange kind of conies', with tails like those of a rat, and the feet of a mole. 'Under his chin, one either side, he (the conie) hath a bag, into which he gathereth his meat, when he hath filled his belly abroad, that he may either feed his young, or feed himself when he lists not to travel from his burrow. The people eat their (the Conies') bodies, and make great account of their skins, for their king's holiday coat was made of them'.

Here they nailed a plate of brass to a strong post, as a testament to them having been there, and also to establish 'Her Majesty's and (Her) successors' right and title to that kingdom...'. (The Spaniards had apparently never ventured this far north.) The inscription, roughly scratched onto the plate of brass, read as follows: 'BEE IT KNOWNE VNTO ALL MEN BY THESE PRESENTS IVNE (June). 17.1579. BY THE GRACE OF GOD AND IN THE NAME OF HERR MAIESTY QVEEN ELIZABETH OF ENGLAND AND HERR SVCCESSORS FOREVER I TAKE POSSESSION OF THIS KINGDOME WHOSE KING AND PEOPLE FREELY RESIGNE THEIR RIGHT AND TITLE IN THE WHOLE LAND VNTO HERR MAIESTIES KEEPEING NOW NAMED BY ME AN TO BEE KNOWNE VNTO ALL MEN AS NOVA ALBION. (General) FRANCIS DRAKE'.

Drake named this country 'New Albion', firstly in respect of the 'white banks and cliffs which lie toward the sea', and secondly 'that it might have some affinity... with our own country'. (In fact 'Albion' is the Old English word for England, or Britain, and derives from the Latin 'albus', meaning 'white', as in the cliffs found there). On July 23, they departed, the natives taking 'a sorrowful farewell' of them.

ை

There has been much speculation and debate as to exactly how far northwards Drake did travel, and exactly where he stopped, from June 17 to July 23, to ground and careen his ship.

Hakluyt states that on June 5 they were at a latitude of 43 degrees, but *The World Encompassed* says that they reached a 'height (latitude) of 48 deg.' (which is between the present-day cities of Vancouver in Canada, and Seattle in the U.S.A.).

As far as the landing is concerned, Hakluyt states that the bay was 'within 38 degrees towards the line (equator)', whereas *The World Encompassed* puts it at '38 deg. 30 min'. According to Hakluyt, having departed, they then 'continued without sight of land till the 13. day of October following...', but this is contradicted by the 'World Encompassed', which may provide a vital clue because according to this account, on July 24 (the day after departure), they reached some islands, 'having on them plentiful and great store of seals and birds...'. These must have been the Farallon Islands, which lie 28 miles west of San Francisco's present-day Golden Gate. Now as these islands are described as being 'not far without this harborough (harbour)...' which was probably either San Francisco Bay, the Bolinas Lagoon, 12 miles to the north-west, or the present-day 'Drake's Bay', 30 miles to the north-west (east of Point Reyes). In favour of Drake's Bay is the presence of white cliffs facing the sea, as described by Hakluyt. Because the islands are mentioned in some accounts and not others however, historian Henry R. Wagner has cast doubt as to whether Drake did actually land there at all! Will the truth ever be known?

The Circumnavigation – From 'New Albion' to Plymouth

The 'extremity of the cold not only continued, but increased', and therefore, having failed to find the fabled Northwest Passage, Drake, 'with the consent of all', set sail across the Pacific on July 25, bound for the Islands of the Moluccas (Indonesia). Even one as determined as he could not prevail against the rigours of that particularly inclement winter. The captured Spanish prize of Rodrigo Tello was left behind. Then, having had no sight of land for sixty-eight days, they reached the Philippine island of Pelew – the voyage having taken them to within 400 miles of the north coast of Australia (a continent yet to be 'discovered' by Europeans, when it was claimed for England by Captain Cook two centuries later).

Here, a great number of canoes came out to greet them but although, as Fletcher states, the people 'entreated us by signs most earnestly to draw nearer to the shore', Drake and his men suspected that they intended 'mischief to us'. Events proved them right, for having discovered that their demands would not be met unless they offered something in return, the natives 'let fly' from the store of stones which they had in their canoes. Drake, as usual, showed great forebearance, being unwilling 'to requite their malice by like injury'. However, so that they might know that he had the 'power to do them harm', he 'caused a great piece to be shot off, not to hurt them, but to afright them'. This had the desired effect, for every single native leaped out of his canoe into the water, dived under the keel of his boat, and stayed there until Drake's ship was 'gone a good way from them'. Drake nicknamed this the 'Island of Thieves'!

Having watered at the Philippine island of Mindanao, on November 3 they reached the Moluccas, which was their goal. As they passed the island of Ternate, an official came out to welcome them in a canoe, and told them that his ruler, Sultan Babur, had found in the Portuguese, 'nothing but deceit and treachery', but he was 'wondrous glad of his (Drake's) coming'.

Drake now learnt that ten years earlier, the Portuguese had invaded the nearby island of Tidore and murdered its ruler, the present Sultan's father, and 'intended the like to all his sons'. Having therefore been forced to abandon the entire island, Sultan Babur and his people had driven the Portuguese out of Ternate, and had relocated themselves there. Since that time, the king had progressively extended his kingdom, which now included 'an hundred islands hereabouts'.

Drake's response was to send the Sultan a present of a velvet cloak, whereupon the Sultan in turn dispatched to Drake's ship three large canoes, containing some of the most eminent people who surrounded him. All were attired 'in white lawn (or cloth of Calecut – cotton cloth, first brought from Calicut in India)' and had above their heads, from one end of the canoe to the other, 'a covering of thin and fine mats, borne up by a frame made of reeds, under which every man sat in order according to his dignity'. The sight of so many 'hoary heads' demonstrated that these were the Sultan's councillors, who advised him in his affairs. Finally the Sultan, accompanied by '6 grave and ancient fathers', approached in his own canoe, and was delighted as the *Golden Hind's* ordnance thundered, and 'trumpets and other instruments of music' were sounded in welcome. Here, they obtained cloves, rice, hens, sugar-cane, a fruit which they called 'figo' (possibly figs), cocoas, and 'a kind of meal which they call sago...'.

Then the Sultan went to a large house, in the grounds of which at least a thousand of his people were gathered, 'with 8 or 10 more grave senators following him'. 'A very rich canopy, (adorned in the middest with embossings of gold)' was borne over him, and he was 'guarded with 12 lances', the points of which were turned downwards. He seated himself in his chair of state, there to receive Drake and his men, and be fanned by a page with 'a very costly fan, richly embroidered and beset with sapphires'.

The Sultan was 'of low voice, temperate in speech, of kingly demeanour, and a Moor (Muslim) by nation'. Attired from waist to ground with 'cloth-of-gold', he was bare-legged, but wore on his feet a pair of shoes 'of cordivant (goat-skin leather), dyed red'. His head was 'finely wreathed in divers rings of plaited gold', and around his neck hung a gold chain. On his left hand he wore a diamond, an emerald, a ruby, and a turky (turquoise), and on his right hand he wore one ring set with 'a big and perfect turky', and another set with 'many diamonds of a smaller size...'. The Moorish religion, said Fletcher, consisted 'much in certain superstitious observations of new moons, and certain seasons, with a rigid and strict kind of fasting'.

After this warm welcome, Drake was granted the freedom of the island, and made a verbal agreement with the Sultan whereby his people undertook to sell their spices only to English merchants. They then set sail again, and found a small island to the south of Celebes where they remained for twenty-six days to repair the ship, which was now 'grown foul for want of trimming', and also her 'casks and vessels for water' which were 'much decayed'. To this end they set up tents on the shore, and also a blacksmith's forge. They were now able to refresh their 'sickly, weak, and decayed bodies', and within a short space of time transform themselves into 'strong, lusty and healthful persons'.

Here the men were astonished to see at night, amongst the trees, 'an infinite swarm of fiery-seeming worms... whose bodies (no bigger than an ordinary fly), did make a show and give such light as if every twig on every tree had been the starry sphere'. There were also numerous crayfish, each so large that it was sufficient to satisfy four hungry men at dinner, 'being a very good and restorative meat...'; hence their christening of the place, 'Crab Island'.

On Crab Island they released two negro prisoners (one taken at Paita and the other at Guatulco), and the negress Maria who was now pregnant (from Zarate's ship *Espirito Santo* when it was captured off the coast of El Salvador). The three were provided with sufficient rice, seeds and means of making a fire for them to form a settlement.[1]

On December 12 they put to sea again, but adverse winds forced them to venture into a region where many shoals lay 'here and there, among the islands'. Then, at 8 o'clock on the evening of January 9, with the ship driving forward in full sail, the *Golden Hind* suddenly became stuck fast on a shoal, with no prospect in Fletcher's words of, 'how anything could be saved, or any person escape alive'. All fell prostrate, said their prayers, and expected every minute for 'the final stroke to be given unto us'.

Drake, as always, led from the front, encouraging his men to bestir themselves and follow his example. By manning the pumps and freeing the ship of water they gained some respite, which Fletcher attributed to the 'extraordinary hand of God'. However, the sound design and immense strength of the double-hulled *Golden Hind*, and the meticulous way she had been maintained throughout the voyage, played no small part in this.

The hope now was to find 'good ground and anchor-hold to seaward...' so that the ship might be hauled off the rock. Drake himself took charge of the sounding, but found that even at one boat's length from the ship, the depth was so great that the sounding weight did not reach the bottom.

The situation was becoming desperate. They had only enough victuals to last a few days, and 'not so much as a cup of cold water was to be had'. The nearest land was 6 leagues away; the ship's boat was able to carry only 20 people with any safety, and in any event, the wind was unfavourable. A second attempt to find an anchor-hold failed and now, despite Drake's cheerful speeches of encouragement, it seemed that all the 58-strong crew could look forward to was a lingering death. In desperation, they began unloading the ship and casting some of her goods into the sea, hoping that by lightening her, she would float off the shoal; this included their 'munition for defence', and 'the very meal for (the) sustenation of our lives'.

It was to no avail until suddenly, after twenty-four hours, the elements took a hand. Thus far, the wind had blown against the broadside of the ship, keeping her upright on the shoal. Now it slackened, and as the tide caused the ship to heel over towards the deep water, her keel was freed. This 'day of deliverance' from the reef on which they had been impaled for twenty hours, was January 10, 1580.

The Fletcher narrative omits to mention how Drake proceeded to punish and humiliate his chaplain for being such a 'doom-monger' during their recent period of misfortune. Fletcher had contributed to the general gloom by announcing that the shipwrecking was divine retribution on 'his general' for his previous execution of Thomas Doughty. According to an anonymous witness, Drake assembled his company, then 'put a lock about one of his (Fletcher's) legs' which was then attached to 'a staple (clasp), knocked fast into the hatches in the forecastle of his ship'.[2] Then, 'sitting cross-legged on a chest, and a pair of pantofles (casual foot slippers) in his hand...' he said, 'Francis Fletcher, I do here excommunicate thee out of ye church of God, and from all the benefits and graces therof, and I denounce thee to the Devil and all his angels.' Drake also 'caused a posy (motto) to be written and bound about Fletcher's arm', and the hapless preacher was told that 'if he removed it, or but once ventured before the mast, he would be hanged. Despite this threat, there was an element of good humour, even pantomine in the proceedings, and a few days later, Drake absolved the errant Fletcher, and reinstated him as preacher![3]

For many days, foul weather and dangerous shoals made it difficult for them to clear the coast of Celebes. At the island of Barativa, they exchanged linen cloth and margaretas (pearls) for 'divers and plentiful fruits'. On March 9, they reached Java, where they exchanged silks and cloth with the king, for cocoa, hens, rice and other victuals. Drake and his men entertained the king with music, and he reciprocated by playing them his 'country music', which was 'of a very strange kind, yet the sound was delightful'. Having been presented with an ox, they now trimmed and washed the ship; which after the long voyage was 'so overgrown with a kind of shell-fish sticking fast unto her' that, 'it hindered her exceedingly, and was a great trouble to her sailing'.

On March 26 they set course for the Cape of Good Hope and, 'without touch of aught but air and water', sighted the coast of Africa fifty-six days later. On June 15 they caught sight of the Cape, but continued to Sierra Leone, the scene of Drake's former slaving expeditions, where they 'watered' in the mouth of the River Tagoine, and found oysters, and lemons (which were prophylactic against scurvy).

By August 22 they were at the latitude of the Canary Islands, and 'with joyful minds and thankful hearts to God', they arrived at Plymouth on September 26, 1580, after a journey lasting two years, ten months and eleven days. Only 59 men remained of her original complement of 85. It had been the longest sea-passage ever undertaken, both in terms of time and distance.

As the clerk proudly recorded in the year 1580 in Plymouth's 'Black Book', 'At Mighelmasse (Michaelmas) this yeare came Mr Frauncis Drake home to Plymouthe from the Southe Seay and mollocus and wasse round about the world and wasse Lacke (absent) towe yeares & thre quarters and brought home great stoore of golde and sylver in blockes. And was afterward in the same yere for his good seruice in thatt behalf done kneighted'.

ᕦᕤ

So how did Drake achieve his great feat of circumnavigating the earth, his *Golden Hind* being only the second ship ever to do so after the *Victoria* (of Magellan's fleet)? Willpower was certainly a factor, yes, and Drake was to expound his philosophy in respect of this in a letter to

Walsingham which he wrote ten years later. 'There must be a beginning of any great matter, but the continuing of it unto the end, until it be thoroughly finished, yields the true glory.' However, other qualities were also required.[4]

The English Channel, and the western coasts of France, Spain and North Africa were familiar to Drake, but when the ship was offshore, and the land 'fell away' until it was out of sight, what then? He undoubtedly carried an 'Astrolabe', which consists of a circular dial, calibrated around the rim in degrees, and with a diametric pointer pivoted at its centre. Suspended freely from above, the pointer was aimed at the sun at dawn or dusk, and the degree of elevation from the horizontal read off from where the shadow fell on the scale. At night, the pole star was used instead, and could be viewed directly through the pointer's sights. Then, from an almanac, the reading could be converted into an estimate of the ship's latitude. The limitations of the method were that it was difficult to take an accurate reading from a rolling ship; and impossible if the weather was cloudy. An error of only one degree was equivalent to being 60 miles off course.

Longitude was another matter, and at that time impossible to determine in the same way using heavenly bodies. The only way it could be measured was by knowing the speed of the ship and the distance travelled. Speed was measured by 'log-line' and knotted rope (speed is still measured in 'knots', even to this day). Direction was shown by the magnetic compass, but the mariner had to bear in mind that magnetic north was not the same as geographical north. The needle, which required periodical recharging with a lodestone, could be affected by any iron contained in the ship, such as in cannon or nails; since iron is spread irregularly throughout the earth's crust, the compass reading could contain an error of up to several degrees, depending on where the ship was on the earth's surface. Finally, time was measured by the 'half-hour glass', which had to be inverted every half-hour when the sand ran out. To upset the calculations, it only required the ship's boy to neglect his duties, or fall asleep in the early hours. The results were plotted by moving pegs on a 'traverse-board' on which were depicted the points of the compass, which was used to record the direction and distance travelled every four-hour watch.

Drake himself was also reputed to have carried an 'astronomical compendium' in the shape of a pocket watch, which included tables of latitude and tides for European ports; a sun-dial, a perpetual calendar in which saint's days and religious festivals were highlighted; and a calculator to determine the ship's latitude from a noonday observation of the elevation of the sun above the horizon. And of course, as well as relying on his instruments, such as they were, to fix his position and plot his course, Drake made full use of pilots and charts captured from Spanish ships.

Finally, if ever a second voyage was attempted it would be useful to have accurate pictures of the newly-discovered coast. To this end, Drake and his cousin John were to be seen on deck in quiet times, entering paintings of the scenes they saw together in their notebooks (known as 'ruffers', from the French 'routier').

The practical matter of keeping the ship afloat on such a journey was a feat in itself. The *Golden Hind* had no great depth of keel, and would have relied upon cannon balls and other ballast to keep her upright. Incapable of sailing close to the wind, she would have been obliged in heavy seas, to steer head-to-wind to avoid rolling over. If she had rolled over, not being self-righting, she would certainly have been lost. Therefore, a huge factor in Drake's success was that he was meticulously careful as regards the regular maintainance and repair of his ship and the ships of his fleet.

As ever on the voyage, Drake's qualities of leadership and courage shone through. He was scrupulously fair to the natives, refusing to take revenge, even when they killed and mutilated some of his best loved men, because he believed that had the natives known that their vistors were Englishmen, and not the hated Spaniards, they would not have behaved in this way.

Drake was unstinting in his concern for the welfare of his men. For example, when one was 'hurt in the face', Drake summoned the injured man, 'lodged him in his owne shipp', 'seet (seated) him at his own table', and 'would not soffer (suffer) him to depart before he was recovered'.[5]

8

Wealth and Recognition; a Return to the Indies

When Drake arrived back at Plymouth in September, 1580, the first question asked of the local fishermen was, 'Is the Queen still living?'. A change of monarch in his absence, particularly if the new incumbent was a Roman Catholic, could have made the Protestant Drake persona non grata. Fortunately for him however, the reply was that Her Majesty was in good health, but that there was much 'pestilence' in the town. Therefore they did not land, but instead anchored near St Nicholas' Island (later known as Drake's Island), whereupon the mayor, John Blitheman, and Drake's wife Mary, came aboard the *Golden Hind*. It would be five years before Drake put to sea again.

Drake dispatched his trumpeter, John Brewer, to London to appraise the Queen of his homecoming. She responded, as John Drake records, by saying he was to come to Court and bring her some samples of his labours. At this, Drake set off, taking 'certain horses laden with gold and silver'. The remainder he left in Plymouth, by order of the Queen, in the custody of local magistrate, Edmund Tremayne, to be stowed securely in Saltash Castle.[1]

Drake arrived at Richmond Palace, London, where he was given a six-hour audience with the Queen. He presented her with a crown encrusted with five emeralds, three of which were almost as long as a little finger, which she flaunted in front of seething Spanish Ambassador Bernardino de Mendoza. She liked Drake's Devonshire accent, was astonished at the riches he had brought back, and was fascinated by his account of the circumnavigation, which he described graphically, with the aid of a map.

When the Spanish Ambassador demanded reparation for the plunders Drake had committed, he was told that Drake, on his voyage, had inflicted no damage either to Spanish subjects or to Spanish territories. In fact, it is believed that not a single Spanish life was lost! The Queen also pointed out that the Spaniards, by ill-treating her subjects and prohibiting commerce, had brought these misfortunes on themselves.

She added that there would therefore be no further discussion with Philip II until she herself was reimbursed for his interference in Ireland, where he had been deliberately fomenting an Irish revolt against English rule. She denied the Spanish claim to the whole continent of America, simply because it had been donated to them by the Pope; and also their power to prevent people of other nations 'from freely navigating that vast ocean: seeing (that) the use of the sea and air is common to all, and neither nature, nor public use, nor custom, permit any possession thereof'.[2]

The treasure was subsequently loaded onto pack horses and taken to Sion House in Richmond, from where a year later, it was removed to the Tower of London. Any reservations Her Majesty may have had regarding Drake's 'piratical activities' were swiftly overcome, in private at any rate, when she learnt of the sheer size of the treasure haul, which was sufficiently large and of such value as to 'fully defray the charge of seven years' wars, prevent and save the common subject from taxes, loans, privy seals (the requirement of Royal grants for personal rights), subsidies, and fifteenths (a tax of 1/15th, formerly imposed on personal property), and give them good advantage against a daring adversary...'.

It included in excess of ten tons of silver and approximately one hundredweight of gold, of which Drake was granted £10,000 in gold by the Queen for himself, and the sum of £8000 for his crew.[3]

For Her Majesty and the other sponsors, this represented a 5000 per cent return on their investment. Equally important was the fact that the supply of gold upon which Spain relied to pay for, amongst other things, her soldiers in the Netherlands had, by Drake's action, been severely diminished. Some of the proceeds of the voyage went to found the Levant Company, out

Queen Elizabeth I, artist unknown.
Photo: National Portrait Gallery, London.

86

of which sprang the East India Company. Drake, with his new found wealth, now purchased a property in London, in Elbow Lane, and was henceforth often to be seen at Court.

The Queen presented Drake with a sword inscribed with the words, 'Whoso striketh at thee, Drake, striketh also at Us'. A measure of the close relationship she had with Drake is revealed by the comments of Spanish Ambassador Mendoza. 'Drake... passes much time with the Queen, by whom he is highly favoured and told how great is the service he had rendered her'; 'The Queen shows extraordinary favour to Drake and never fails to speak to him when she goes out in public, conversing with him a long time'; 'The Queen often has him in her cabinet, often indeed walking with him in the garden'.

෧෨

In the spring of 1581 the *Golden Hind* sailed on a triumphant voyage from her home port of Plymouth, around the coast and up the River Thames to Deptford, where Drake dressed his ship with great banners painted in gold on silk damask and bearing the Lion of England and the fleur-de-lis of France, a reminder that the Tudors still laid claim to French territory. Here, on April 4, the Queen and her entourage arrived amidst great pomp and ceremony for a banquet.

Elizabeth boarding the Golden Hind, *from a picture by Frank Brangwyn, A.R.A.*
Photo: Whereabouts unknown.

87

The Queen inspected the *Golden Hind* (against the great mast of which were attached laudatory verses, '... composed to the praise and honour of Sir Francis Drake...', some, in Latin, having been written by a scholar of Winchester College) and when she saw the Bible that 'Sir Francis had (taken with) him about ye worlde', she inscribed the title page of it with her own hand.[4] Then, on the Queen's orders, the ship was put on permanent display in a dry dock dug into the river bank, 'as a monument for all posterity'.

Drake was now to be knighted. Instead of performing the ceremony herself, the Queen handed the gilded sword to the Marquis de Marchaumont, Duke Henry of Anjou's representative in England. A delegation was shortly to arrive from France to decide the terms of a proposed marriage treaty between Elizabeth and Henry.

The occasion was not without humour. Drake, knowing the Queen's nickname for Henry her intended was 'The Frog', had mischievously given her the present of a frog encrusted with diamonds. He presented the Queen with a written account of the voyage and an accompanying map. He also gave her a large silver coffer and had made for her a crown, inset with five Peruvian emeralds worth 20,000 crowns, which she would wear on New Year's Day. Drake was also lavish with his gifts to the Queen's councillors; all of whom accepted his presents (totalling 1200 crowns), with the exception of Lord Burghley and Henry Radcliffe, Earl of Sussex.

The Queen in turn, as Drake was kneeling to be knighted, joked that she intended to punish him for turning pirate by striking off his head! Instead, she presented him with a pendant jewel enclosing a miniature portrait of herself by the Devonshire artist Nicholas Hilliard. She also gave him a scarf of green silk, edged with gold lace and embroidered with the motto 'The Almighty be your Guide and your Protector to the End'.

Sir Francis Drake's Coat of Arms, Buckland Abbey.
Photo: National Trust.

Prior to his being knighted, Drake had always used on public and private documents the crest of the Tavistock Drakes, an eagle displayed (with feathers spread). Now the Queen conferred on him a coat of arms with globe, galleon, crest, and motto, *Sic Parvis Magna* – 'Thus much from little'. From that time forth, he used the arms the Queen had given to him, quarterly with the 'waver dragon' (or 'wyvern', which differs from an ordinary dragon in that it has no hind legs), which he was entitled to use by virtue of his kinship with the Drakes of Ashe (near Axminster).

∽

While Drake had been away circumnavigating the world, events at home had moved on. John Hawkins' expeditions to Africa and the New World had made him a wealthy man. He became a Member of Parliament and was known at Court, where he numbered amongst his friends, William Cecil, 1st Baron Burghley, who was Lord Treasurer and Chief Advisor to the Queen.

In the autumn of 1573, Hawkins succeeded his father-in-law, Benjamin Gonson as Treasurer to the Navy, and he soon became its comptroller also. He was charged with the development and mainte-nance of the Queen's fleet, and was to oversee many of the improve-ments to the design of Her Majesty's warships. The main credit for this, however, must go to ship designers Matthew Baker and Peter Pett from the Navy Board.

The result was the racing galleon. Ships were now made longer, and therefore faster. They also became more efficient; since by lowering the previously huge forecastles and sterncastles, they could sail closer to the wind. The size of the ships' crews was also reduced. This enabled them to remain at sea for four or even six months at a time without revict-ualling.

There had also been problems in Ireland where, in the summer of 1579, the exiled nationalist leader, Sir James Fitzmaurice Fitzgerald, landed at the Dingle peninsula in the south-west with a force of Spanish and Italian mercenaries, supported by the Pope. This occurrence served further to increase the tension between England and Spain. With Fitzgerald's brother, the Earl of Desmond's help, the province of Munster fell into rebel hands, but seaborne operations by the

Government led to the defeat of the rebels, and the death of Fitzgerald. The same fate befell reinforcements which landed in Smerwick harbour on the Dingle peninsula the following September.

The English army on that occasion included a young Devon-born captain named Walter Raleigh, who was some twelve years younger than Sir Francis Drake. An experienced seafarer, Raleigh had sailed to the Azores two years earlier as captain of the *Falcon*, in a fleet commanded by Sir Humphrey Gilbert. Now he would have no scruples about implementing the Lord Deputy Grey's order to put the six hundred rebels to the sword.

A few months later, Raleigh was at Court, where he quickly made friends with Robert Dudley, the Earl of Leicester.

The death of King Sebastian of Portugal, who was killed in Morocco in the battle of Alcazar-el-Kebir in August, 1578, marked the end of Christian attempts to conquer Moorish (Mohammedan) North Africa. Sebastian was succeeded by his sixty-seven-year-old great-uncle, Cardinal Henry. When, two years later, he too died, King Philip of Spain laid claim to the Portuguese throne. The Duke of Alva was summoned out of retirement to command the King's forces which, on June 27, 1580, crossed the border. On August 25, the Spaniards raised their flag on the battlements of Lisbon's Royal Palace, and the pretender to the Portuguese throne, Duke Braganza and Antonio, Prior of Crato (who was the illegitimate son of the brother of the late cardinal King Henry), was driven out. When Oporto fell in the October, this marked the end of the campaign.

Now, to the Empire of Spain was added that of Portugal, namely the East Indies, with its silks and spices; West Africa, with its gold and slaves; Brazil and Madeira, with their fine timber; and the Cape Verde Islands which now provided a provisioning base for the Indies fleets.

Of equal importance were the 11 magnificent ocean-going galleons which fell into Philip's hands, together with their seaports and seamen. This surpassed anything which he himself possessed, and formed the nucleus of his navy.

Buckland Abbey.

In November, 1580, Drake negotiated the purchase of Buckland Abbey, (originally a Cistercian monastery founded in 1278 by Amicia, Countess of Devon) together with its household furnishings and estates, from Sir Richard Grenville, for the sum of £3400. Grenville, cousin of Walter Raleigh, was of a Cornish family. His father, Sir Roger, had captained the warship *Mary Rose*, and had gone down with his ship when she heeled over and sank on July 15, 1545, in full view of the King, Henry VIII, whilst attempting to frustrate an attempt by the fleet of French King Francis I to invade England.

At Buckland Abbey, Drake had the dining room panelled, and displayed his new coat of arms above the fireplace. Around its carved oak table the battle plan for the defeat of the Spanish Armada would one day be conceived!

To reach Plymouth from his new home, Drake would have taken the long, narrow track through the hamlet of Milton Combe, down the valley to Lopwell on his beloved River Tavy, where he had fished as a boy. Here, from the quay, he would have sailed on the tide to the River

Tamar; then down the Hamoaze anchorage into Plymouth Sound, and from there to Sutton Pool on the east side of the Hoe (a 'Hoe' being a promontory), the traditional place of mooring for the ships. This was the same route as had been formerly used by the monks of the abbey.

In September, 1581, Drake was elected mayor of Plymouth, with a yearly stipend of £20. He purchased from his uncle, William Hawkins, 40 properties in Plymouth; mainly residential but also including warehouses, a bakehouse and a vault (cellar). At the same time, he continued to expand his maritime interests.[5]

New Year was the time when it was customary for the Queen to receive gifts from her courtiers, and in 1582 Drake is believed to have presented her with a pendant jewel of gold, pearls and enamel in the shape of a ship, with accompanying tiny gold boat as a hanging drop. She in turn presented him with a parchment illuminated with birds, fruit, and flowers, embossed with the great initial letter 'E', and inscribed with the words, 'Whereas Sir Francis Drake, Kt, had circumnavigated the globe from east to west, and had discovered in the south part of the world many unknown places, Her Majesty, to perpetuate his fame and valour, did grant unto him and his heirs all the manor of Sherford (near Kingsbridge) in Devonshire...'. She also bestowed on him other properties and lands in Northumberland, Durham and Yorkshire.

෨ඃ

On May 1, 1582, a fleet of four ships was sent to Calicut on the coast of Malabar in equatorial Guinea, with the purpose of establishing an English outpost for trade with the Moluccas. One of the ships, the *Francis*, was owned by Drake who was currently serving as mayor of Plymouth. The ship was captained by his cousin and erstwhile page, John Drake. The expedition was not a success, the *Francis* ran aground in the Rio de la Plata; its crew was captured by Indians. John Drake (with crewmember Richard Fairweather) eventually fell into the clutches of the Spaniards, was tried by the Inquisition, imprisoned for many years, and condemned to remain on Spanish territory for the remainder of his life. These facts would not become known to Sir Francis Drake until September, 1587.

In the summer of 1582, seven vessels provided and armed by Drake, were preparing to sail for Terciera in the Azores, to be followed by three more in the autumn. Late in 1582, Drake contributed two ships to a fleet which sailed successfully to the West Indies, returning the following year with pearls, hides, sugar and treasure.

Drake, who was by no means universally popular at Court, had an implacable enemy in John Doughty, brother of Thomas. Having failed to have Drake brought to trial for the murder of his brother, Doughty made constant complaints against him. However, when under torture, an English merchant named Patrick Mason implicated Doughty as a spy, the latter was interned in the Marshalsay (a prison in Southwark, governed by the marshal of the royal household), and as far as is known, was never released.

In the summer of 1582, Drake purchased part of the manor of Yarcombe (near Honiton) from his friend and kinsman, Richard Drake (younger brother of Sir Bernard Drake of Ashe, who was soon to become equerry to the Queen). In the New Year, Drake gave his customary gift to the Queen, an elaborate salt-cellar in the shape of a globe, with images of the classical gods of mythology, Jupiter and Pallas.

Drake's wife Mary, who became Lady Drake when her husband was knighted, died in January 1583, and was buried in Plymouth on the 25 of that month in the same Church of St Budeaux where they had been married. There were no offspring from the marriage, despite its thirteen-year duration. Drake had, however, previously assumed responsibility for Lady Drake's nephew, Jonas Bodenham, who was left destitute when his father died during his infancy. In that year, Drake was elected member of a Commission charged with the efficient maintenance of the Royal Navy.

In 1584 Drake became Member of Parliament for Bossiney in north Cornwall, and was a member of the committee involved in drawing up the act for supplying Plymouth with water.

૭૦

Don Antonio, pretender to the throne of Portugal, made an attempt to establish himself in the Azores; the sole possession of the old Portuguese Empire which had not yielded to Philip's annexation of 1580. In this, he was assisted by Catherine de Medici, widow of Henry II of France, and the French fleet commanded by Filippo Strozzi. The attempt was a failure, and in June, 1583, the French were roundly defeated at Terciera (largest island in the Azores) by the Spaniards under Don Alvaro de Bazan, Marquis of Santa Cruz and Captain General of the Ocean Sea; after which Philip gained control of the Azores. On September 7, 1585, Don Antonio arrived at Plymouth, 'verye poore...' and was sent for by Her Majesty Queen Elizabeth to her 'Corte, where he was condocted with 50 horses or more'.[6]

In 1585, Drake married Elizabeth, only daughter and heiress of the wealthy Sir George Sydenham of Combe Sydenham in Somerset. Now he was possessed not only of great material wealth, but also of an aristocratic wife. Again, the marriage produced no offspring, which is curious, considering how prolific his late father Edmund had been in this respect! It is unlikely that both his first and his second wife were unable to bear children; so the conclusion must be either that Drake was infertile, or that he had homosexual tendencies.

৩৩

Although they were both Devonians and staunch Protestants, Walter Raleigh was in many ways the opposite of Drake. Six feet tall, a poet and scholar, his magnificent costumes were acquired 'to the utmost limit of his purse'.[7] Raleigh had served in France in 1569, as a volunteer in the Huguenot army, and had been present at the battles of Jarnac and Moncontour. In 1578 he commanded the *Falcon* as vice admiral to Sir Humphrey Gilbert, setting sail across the Atlantic on a so-called 'voyage of discovery' in which virtually nothing substantive was achieved.

In February, 1580, Raleigh served in Ireland (where he was captain of a company of 100 soldiers) on a commission which sentenced James

Elizabeth Sydenham, painted in 1585, around the time of her marriage to Drake.
Photo: City of Plymouth Museums and Art Gallery.

94

Fitzgerald to death as a traitor. In the November he carried out the orders of Lord Deputy Arthur Grey and put to the sword 600 of the Spanish and Italian adventurers who had invaded that country.

Raleigh became a firm favourite of the Queen, who showered him with gifts, including vast tracts of land in Ireland, and trading monopolies in wine and wool. These brought him in an income of up to £2000 a year. In 1584 he was knighted, and in 1585 appointed vice admiral of Devon and Cornwall. However, his Achilles' heel was his poor judgement; this would one day cost him his life!

Whilst a student at Oxford, Raleigh had become acquainted with Thomas Harriot, a mathematician who later trained his sea-captains in the art of navigation. This was to be most useful, for it was Raleigh's dream to establish a colony in North America. To this end he used his newly acquired wealth to fit out a 200 ton vessel, the *Bark Raleigh*, which sailed in April, 1584 with two of Harriot's former pupils in navigation, Philip Amadas and Arthur Barlow, as expedition leaders. Having discovered the island of Roanoke (in present-day North Carolina), and claimed it and the adjacent mainland for the Queen, they returned home, bringing with them two of the local Indians. By painstaking inter-rogation of these two Indians over a period of several months, Harriot was able to create an alphabet for the speech sounds of their language, Algonkian, and also to become fluent in it himself.

On their return to England, the Queen in consequence gave the name 'Virginia' to the whole eastern seaboard of North America, from Florida to Newfoundland (after her self-styled title, 'the Virgin Queen').

Raleigh's, however, was not the first English colony to be established in North America. Credit for this goes to the Suffolk born explorer, Bartholomew Gosnold, who created a settlement in 1607 which led to the foundation of Jamestown (Virginia). An investigation is currently taking place to see whether a grave discovered inside the fort is his (Gosnold died in 1607).

In April, 1585, another expedition was despatched; this time under the command of Raleigh's cousin, Sir Richard Grenville, with Harriot as surveyor, and Amadus as admiral of the proposed new colony's boats and pinnaces. Also present was John White, the draughtsman and watercolour artist, who had sailed with Frobisher to the Arctic in 1577 and painted the Eskimos, their kayaks and the ice floes. Having arrived at Roanoke, 100 or more would-be settlers, all male, were put ashore under the governorship of Ralph Lane, a former soldier who had served in Ireland and was an expert in creating fortifications.

❦

When a fleet of English ships went to Spain at the invitation of Philip II, laden with corn for the relief of his famished provinces, the king treacherously seized them, imprisoned their crews, and used the grain to victual the great fleet which he was assembling at Cadiz for a proposed invasion of England.

The Queen responded by assembling a fleet of 24 ships and barks, and 20 pinnaces, whose purpose would be 'to revenge the wrongs offered her, and to resist the King of Spain's preparations (for war)'. The Queen also promised to assist the Netherlands in their struggle for independence from Spain.[8]

Drake, sailing for the first time as a commissioned admiral of the Queen, would command the expedition. The investors, who included the Queen, Drake himself, the Earl of Leicester, John and William Hawkins and Sir Walter Raleigh, would share the profits. Their mandate was to sack and destroy the defences of Spain's Atlantic and Caribbean ports, and to release any English ships found there. It was even envisaged that Drake might hold and garrison one such port permanently, and use it as a base to intercept the homeward-bound Spanish treasure fleet.

Drake sailed as admiral of the Queen's ship, the 600 ton *Elizabeth Bonaventure*, and Martin Frobisher, his vice admiral, sailed as captain of the 300 ton *Primrose*. Rear admiral was Francis Knollys in the *Leicester*; Christopher Carleill in command of the *Tiger*, was lieutenant general of the land forces. The latter, including the sailors, numbered in excess of 3000 men. Carleill, the son-in-law of Sir Francis Walsingham, the Queen's principal secretary, had fought in the Netherlands assisting the Dutch.

❦

FROBISHER.

Martin Frobisher, born in Yorkshire in 1535, was five years older than Sir Francis Drake and up until now had had an adventurous, if somewhat unprofitable career. As an orphan, he became the ward of Sir John York, Master of the Mint and a merchant of the Muscovy Company, trading with Russia, who sent him to sea.

In August, 1553, when the ships *Lion* and *Primrose* sailed from Plymouth to the Gold Coast, only 40 of the 140 crew survived the voyage. One of them was the eleven-year-old Frobisher. The remainder succumbed to fever. After this, the youth spent some years sailing to the Levant (Eastern Mediterranean) and North Africa.

A virtual illiterate who could barely write his name, Frobisher was a man of immense determination and physical strength. He also became an accomplished navigator. In June, 1576, the Queen granted him a licence to cross the Atlantic and search for a north-west passage around North America to Cathay (China) and Zipanu (Japan). Were it to be discovered, such a passage would cut several thousands of miles off the journey around Cape Horn. Also, ships would be able to sail free from the danger of foreign princes and pirates.

As captain of the *Gabriel*, Frobisher sailed in company with another bark of 25 tons and a smaller vessel, around the southern extremity of Greenland and on up the coast of Labrador, where they encountered icebergs as high as the masts of their ships. He missed the entrance to Hudson Bay, but discovered a long inlet at the southern tip of Baffin Island, which he named 'Frobisher Strait' (now Frobisher Bay).

Local Eskimos were eager to trade their salmon and seal meat for looking-glasses, bells and other trinkets; but the atmosphere soured when five of Frobisher's men went ashore and were not seen again. At this, Frobisher took hold of a kayak (seal-skin canoe) and lifted it bodily into the *Gabriel*, whereupon the astonished Eskimo, who happened to be in the kayak at the time, bit off his tongue in astonishment! They took the Eskimo with them back to England, but he died there of a cold!

On his return, Frobisher announced (mistakenly) that he had found the fabled north-west passage, and put on display 200 tons of black ore which he had collected from Baffin Island. Rumours quickly circulated that this contained gold, and Frobisher's discovery precipitated a 'gold-rush'. However, the 'gold' was in fact pyrites (sulphide of iron) – quite worthless – and many investors, the Queen included, lost their money.

On May 20, 1577, Frobisher sailed from Blackwall near Greenwich on the River Thames, as captain of Her Majesty's 180 ton ship the *Aide*, with '100 men of all sorts...', of whom '30 or moe (more) were Gentlemen and

Souldiers, the rest sufficient and tall Sailers'. They took with them supplies to last for half a year. Frobisher, on his return to England, once again reported to the Queen that he had discovered gold in abundance.[9]

This prompted a third voyage by Frobisher in 1578, during the course of which the ship *Salamander* struck a whale; she did so with such force that she stopped dead in the water. The 100 ton *Bark Dennis* struck an iceberg and sank rapidly, but Frobisher survived both the storms and the ice which threatened to entrap his vessels. He returned to England with little to show for his efforts; after which the Queen forbad further expeditions to this inhospitable region of the world.

Frobisher was to become an outspoken critic of Drake, and yet when the real showdown with Spain came in 1588, it was he who had to be extricated, on more than one occasion, from dangerous situations of his own making.

Drake and his fleet set sail on September 14, 1585. Off the coast of Spain they captured a merchant ship, and having ascertained that it was crewed by Catholics and probably heading for Spain, Drake claimed it as a prize. After rounding Cape Finisterre, seven French ships were sighted and one, which was new, was pressed into the fleet.

On September 27, the fleet anchored in the mouth of the River Vigo in north-west Spain, and occupied the town. This was largely a propaganda exercise by which the King of Spain would be insulted, and the beleaguered Dutch and Huguenots in the Netherlands and France given encouragement. Drake now threatened to attack the nearby town of Bayonna, unless English ships and sailors were released from the embargo imposed on them by Spain.

A storm blew three of Drake's ships out to sea; when they returned he noticed that boats were leaving Vigo and taking goods upriver. A raiding party sent in pursuit captured wine, sugar, and the silver cross and vestments from Vigo's cathedral which the Spaniards had hoped to carry away to safety.

An English raiding party pillaged properties in and around the town to the value of 30,000 ducats following which terms were agreed whereby Drake was allowed to replenish his stores and take on water; English prisoners were to be released from prison; and Drake would return (or compensate for the theft of) the stolen goods. However, there is no evidence that compensation was ever paid, and the fleet put to sea again on October 11.

Drake was unfortunate in that he failed to intercept both Spanish treasure fleets, the one reaching the port of San Lucar on September 22, and the other the Azorean island of Terceira on October 7. From Vigo Drake sailed to the Canaries, reaching the island of Palma on November 2. Here, a barrage of cannon fire from its fortress forced him to sail on, several of his ships having been hit.

Anxious about a lack of discipline shown by his men in the attack on Vigo, Drake issued orders concerning their conduct. 'What person soever shall wander or strag(g)le from his ensigne without command-ment shall receue (receive) punishment according to the law of armes, to wit death...'. No man should 'offer to take any pilladge (pillage) or make any spoyle before proclamation made uppon payne of death...', or 'retayne or kepe to himselfe any gould (gold), siluer (silver), Iewellry (jewelry), or any thinge of special price...'. In a gesture of conciliation, he signed the order, 'Youre loving Frende, F. Drake'.[10]

Having reached the Canary island of Hierro on November 5, and found some plunder there, Drake then sailed to Santiago, capital of the Cape Verde Islands (in the eastern Atlantic, 500 miles west of Senegal). Here, Carleill, commander of the soldiers, landed with a party of 600 men, including harquebusiers and longbowmen, to attack the town, where they found a plentiful supply of gunpowder and victuals. A new caravel (small sailing ship) was requisitioned and added to the fleet.

Two men were hanged; one for murdering an officer, and the other for committing sodomy with two of the ship's boys. Drake was evidently unsure about the loyalty of his men, for he demanded that everybody, from highest officer to lowest ranker, take an oath of fealty (fidelity). When Francis Knollys, captain of the *Galleon of Leicester*, refused to take the oath, he was relieved of his command. Having burned the nearby town of Santo Domingo, and then gone on to burn Sao Tiago itself, Drake set sail again on November 28.

The fleet was only a few days out when it was struck by an epidemic of plague, contracted presumably in the Cape Verde Islands. The treat-ment advised by Drake was bleeding; nevertheless between two and three hundred men died as a result of it.

The West Indian island of Dominica was reached on December 18, and on January 1, 1586, the island of Hispaniola, literally 'little Spain' (now Haiti/Dominican Republic). The occupation of its principal city, Santo Domingo, was not achieved without difficulty, since although its militia were poorly armed and trained, the harbour was protected by a sandbank on which several ships had been scuttled to make entry even more problematical. Drake therefore landed Carleill and his troops at a nearby beach to westward, from where they marched on and captured the city. This enabled the fleet to enter the inner harbour in safety.

At Santo Domingo, Drake was able to exchange two of his own ships, the *Benjamin* and the *Scout*, which were leaking, for a merchant ship of 400 tons. He also took a 200 ton vessel, and named the two additions *New Year's Gift* and *New Hope*. When the Spaniards failed to pay the ransom which he demanded, Drake's men began burning and looting the town. In the 'audienca' building (court of justice), Drake captured an escutchion (shield, on which a coat of arms is represented), bearing the motto of King Philip of Spain: *Non Sufficit Orbis* ('The world is not enough'). Finally, having accepted the disappointing sum of 25,000 ducats, which included jewelery given up by the women, and plate from the cathedral, Drake sailed away.

During the occupation of Santo Domingo, a Spanish soldier appeared on horseback carrying a flag of truce. When Drake sent a negro boy to find out what he wanted, the Spaniard ran the boy through with his pike staff. Drake was so incensed by this that he promptly hanged two friars, who were prisoners of his, at the very spot where the boy had been killed, and threatened to hang two more prisoners every day until the culprit was identified. Drake considered it 'a more honourable revenge to make them (the Spaniards) there, in our sight, perform the execution (of the Spanish officer) themselves, which was done accordingly'.

Cartagena, in Colombia, was regarded as the capital of the Spanish Main. Its harbour was in a great lagoon, which was separated from the open sea by a sand spit, on which were sited ramparts and gun batteries. The fleet entered the lagoon, and while Frobisher, in a diversionary raid, feinted to attack, Carleill and his men landed on the sand spit during the night. Avoiding the covering fire of two Spanish galleys, Carleill's men took the town after vigorous hand to hand fighting with sword and pike.[11]

When Martin Frobisher's attack on the fort was driven off, his pinnaces returned to the fleet carrying the dead and wounded. At this failure, Drake became angry, and was determined that he himself would succeed, where his colleague Frobisher had failed. When his seaborne attack suffered the same fate, Drake landed 200 men on the sand spit and captured a cannon, which he set up on the wharf and turned against the defenders.

After this bombardment, the battery was captured and the commander, Captain Alonso Bravo wounded and taken prisoner. Indian archers fired poisoned arrows, but to little avail, as Carleill's men were well protected with armour. As the Spanish galleys attempted to leave the harbour and came under fire from the English pinnaces, a barrel of gunpowder on one of them exploded, whereupon its galley slaves, having been unchained, fled into the countryside. Both galleys were then driven ashore. The cost to the English was in excess of 100 lives, and there were now only 700 men left fit for duty and the defence of the town.

Acrimonious negotiations then took place between Drake and the local governor and bishop over the amount of ransom to be paid. These went on for several weeks, during which time Drake systematically destroyed the city, including the newly constructed cathedral. Finally, the Spaniards agreed to pay the sum of 110,000 ducats.

Drake left Cartagena on March 31, but returned within two days when the *New Year's Gift* began to leak severely. Her cargo of cannons, captured at Santo Domingo, had then to be unloaded and distributed amongst the remainder of the fleet. Drake could have attempted to hold Cartagena, the collection point for the gold, pearls and sugar of the Spanish Main, but his greater ambition was to capture Panama, depot for the Peruvian treasure which was of infinitely greater value. However, the 'calentura' (burning fever) had taken such a toll that he no longer possessed suffi-cient manpower for the task.

On April 14, Drake set sail for the Cayman Islands, where his men shot some alligators for meat. From here they sailed to Cabo de San Antonio, the westernmost point of Cuba, where they found a frigate which they set on fire.

At Havana, the assembly point for the treasure fleet returning to Spain, they came under fire and were forced to anchor in the nearby Guacuranao River. Sailing northwards, they reached the Florida port of San Agustin on May 27. However, having been forewarned, the popula-tion of the town had been evacuated, and Drake was able to enter it unopposed. Here was plunder in the form of guns and tools, and a chest containing 6000 ducats. A small vessel was added to the fleet, replacing another vessel captured off Havana. During a skirmish with Spanish troops retreating from a nearby log fort, Drake's sergeant major, Captain Anthony Powell, was killed; this may have prompted him to show no restraint when he reduced the port to rubble.

Continuing northwards along the coast of Virginia, Drake was attracted by a signal beacon at Croatoan Island, occupied by English settlers deposited there the previous year by Sir Walter Raleigh. The enterprise had not been a success. There was a lack of warm clothing and appropriate agricultural implements, and many of the settlers, being drawn from the gentry or professional classes, were unused to the manual labour that was required to build houses and grow crops. Drake found the governor, Ralph Lane, demoralised, in desperate need of supplies, and anxious for a ship to be provided in which he and his companions might return home. Drake duly obliged, and offered him the *Francis*. However, a hurricane blew the fleet from its anchorage, and the *Francis* was never seen again; whereupon the settlers sailed back to England with Drake.

In the meantime, Raleigh had sent Grenville out again to the Roanoke colony with more settlers and supplies. When Grenville found the place deserted, he returned home, leaving 15 men behind as a token presence.

Drake reached Plymouth on July 28, 1586, carrying what is believed to be England's first supply of tobacco and potatoes. He had kept no records of the accounts, and his claim for expenses of £60,400 was considered excessive. Nevertheless the Queen was delighted with the enterprise and ordered Drake's promotion to the rank of admiral.

Of the 1925 men who had sailed with Drake, 750 had been lost, and the profits were insufficient to pay the survivors' wages. Nonetheless, Drake had captured no less than 240 great guns, which to the Spaniards were a precious commodity, for being unable to manufacture them themselves, they were forced to rely on imports from Italy, or even from England on the black market. Even the venerable Lord Treasurer Burghley, not a friend of Drake, was forced to admit, 'Truly Sir Francis Drake is a fearful man to the King of Spain!'[12]

Meanwhile at Court, Robert Devereux, 2nd Earl of Essex and stepson of Robert Dudley, came to the notice of Queen Elizabeth. He was aged twenty-one when he returned to England in 1587, having been a soldier in the Netherlands. Petulant and prone to rages, Devereux went too far when he raised a rebellion against his sovereign, which left her with no alternative but to have him tried for treason. Elizabeth revealed how deep her feelings were for Devereux when, having signed his death warrant, she sat in her chamber and wept.

In the summer of 1587, Raleigh sent a larger expedition to Roanoke, which this time included both men and women, with John White as governor. However, when supplies ran short, White returned home, leaving 89 men, 17 women and two children, including his own daughter and her child, behind. All these would-be colonists subsequently disappeared without trace.

The Queen now lost confidence in Raleigh, who had been eclipsed by the dazzling exploits of Sir Francis Drake. Therefore, although Raleigh was a courtier, his ambition of becoming a member of the influential Privy Council remained unfulfilled. In short, she no longer trusted his judgement.

9

A Polarisation of Forces – the Raid on Cadiz

Over the years there were many conspiracies by Mary Stuart to supplant Elizabeth, and have herself placed on the English throne. One such plot involved Francis Throckmorton, nephew of Sir Nicholas Throckmorton, a former ambassador to France and Scotland. Having been caught in the act of sending a cipher to Mary, Throckmorton was tortured and executed. The government then took drastic action and in January 1584, Spanish Ambassador Mendoza was expelled from the country. In May, Philip suddenly seized all English ships trading in Spanish ports.

In early 1585, Mary, having been moved from one place of incarceration to another in the sixteen years since her first imprisonment, was again transferred to Tutbury. In April she was placed in the custody of the unsmiling puritan, Sir Amyas Paulet, who kept her under close observation, whilst permitting her to venture out on horse riding excursions.

In January 1586, Mary was transferred to neighbouring Chartley Manor, where she found a method of communicating secretly, or so she thought, with her supporters. Letters sent and received by her travelled in sealed, watertight containers, which were placed in the bung-holes of the beer casks delivered to and from the house. What Mary did not know was that both her servant and the brewer of the beer were in the pay of Elizabeth's chief spymaster, Sir Francis Walsingham.

Mary received one such letter which gave details of a plot to murder Elizabeth and place herself on the throne of England. It was sent to her by a wealthy merchant by the name of Anthony Babington; he had become infatuated with her, having served as her page in the early years of her imprisonment. The 'usurper Elizabeth' would be 'dispatched', the Spaniards would invade, and Mary would then seize Elizabeth's throne.[1] Mary replied to Babington with words of encouragement; when these letters were intercepted by the authorities, Elizabeth's patience finally ran out and Mary's fate was sealed.

On September 5, Babington and his accomplices were tried, convicted of having designs against the life of the Queen, and executed. On September 25, Mary was transferred to Fotheringhay Castle in Northamptonshire where she was tried and found guilty. She was unrepentant. 'Oh weep not,' she said, 'for you shall shortly see Mary Stuart at the end of all her sorrows. You shall report that I dye (die) true and constant in my religion, and firm in my love to Scotland and to France.'[2]

Elizabeth agonised long and hard over signing Mary's death warrant; but was finally persuaded to do so by Charles Howard, the Lord Admiral. On February 8, 1587, Mary was beheaded in the Great Hall of Fotheringhay Castle. After her death, Elizabeth donned mourning garments and wept, possibly more through fear of the consequences than through any attachment to Mary, who had been her prisoner for almost nineteen years, although the two had never met. Mary was buried in Peterborough Cathedral. In 1612, she was reburied at Westminster Abbey.

With the execution of Mary Stuart, war with Spain became inevitable. Not only was Philip of Spain enraged, but so too was James VI of Scotland, Mary's son. James was only appeased by an offer of the prospect of succession to the English Crown. However, seeing the execution of Mary Stuart as a provocation too far, Philip prepared to launch his 'invincible' Armada.

๑๑

In 1555 the Netherlands had passed to Spain on the division of the Hapsburg Empire. However, a revolt by the Dutch Protestants caused King Philip, in 1567 to order an army under the Duke of Alva to restore order in that country.

In that same year, William, Prince of Orange was elected stadholder (viceroy) of the United Dutch Provinces (the so-called States General), and on July 9, Sir Humphrey Gilbert from England landed at Flushing with a force of volunteers to support William's 'rebels'. In November 1572 Gilbert was recalled and in 1573, in a gesture of reconciliation with Spain, with whom she had no desire to go to war, Elizabeth expelled the Dutch 'Sea Beggars' from English ports, from where they had launched attacks on Spanish ships. This led to the restoration of trade with Spain.

105

In the same year Don Luis de Requesens y Cuniga, Grand Commander of Castile, succeeded Alva as Governor. When he died in 1575 and the provinces were left to be governed by a council of state, the occupying Spanish troops (who had not been paid), went on the rampage and ransacked town after town, including Antwerp, then the wealthiest city in Europe.

In November 1575, a new governor was sent, Don Juan of Austria, an illegitimate son of the Emperor Charles V of Spain, and hero of the battle of Lepanto (Greece, 1571, in which combined Western fleets broke the power of the muslim Ottoman Empire). In 1577, diplomatic relations between England and Spain were resumed.

William of Orange turned to Elizabeth, a fellow Protestant, for help. Elizabeth was anxious to avoid offending Spain, but nevertheless she responded by covertly providing him with gold. In March, 1578 Sir John Norris of England was sent with 2000 men, to assist Prince William. Nevertheless, Don Juan succeeded in forcibly separating the southern provinces (Flanders, Artois, Hainault, Namur, Limburg, Luxemburg, Liege, and part of Gelderland and Brabant – now Holland) from the Dutch provinces in the north (Zeeland, Utrecht, Friesland, Groningen, Overyssel, Zutphen and part of Gelderland and Brabant – now Belgium) and uniting them with Spain. However, on October 1 he died and was succeeded by Alexander Farnese, Prince (later Duke) of Parma. Farnese, Spain's ablest general, was another illegitimate son of Emperor Charles V, and his mother Margaret was Regent of the Netherlands.

William also enlisted the support of Francis, Duke of Anjou and brother and heir to the French King Henry III. Francis was seen as an ideal suitor for Elizabeth, and such a union would have given England a powerful ally on the continent. However, in 1584, before the marriage plans could be put into effect, Francis died, having failed to defeat the Spanish in the Low Countries.

On July 10, 1584, William of Orange was murdered by a Catholic fanatic at his family home in Delft. This left Elizabeth as the only remaining Protestant leader in Europe.

In September 1585, Elizabeth despatched an army of 7000 men, commanded by Robert Dudley to the Low Countries. Dudley's arrival was greeted with much pomp and circumstance; so much so that the States General offered him absolute governorship of the United

Provinces. This he accepted, much to the annoyance of the Queen, whose permission he had not obtained.

Having conducted an unsuccessful campaign against the Prince of Parma, Dudley returned home a year later, only to be sent back again with a message for the Dutch telling them that they must come to terms with Spain. Dudley then resigned from his governorship and returned to England.

∾

CADIZ.

By November 1586, the relationship with the Dutch had changed to the extent that Drake, in a show of support for Dom Antonio, pretender to the throne of Portugal, was dispatched to Holland to enlist their help in a proposed joint naval expedition against Spain's American colonies. However, negotiations proved fruitless, and instead he spent the spring of 1587 patrolling the Channel.

The Queen and her Council, having been informed of 'a mightie preparation by Sea begunne in Spaine for the invasion of England... thought it expedient to prevent the same'. Preparations went ahead without the Dutch, and the Queen, 'caused a Fleete of some 30 sailes to be rigged and furnished with all things necessary. Over that Fleete she appointed Generall Sir Francis Drake, to whom she caused 4 ships of her Navie royall to be delivered'.[3] These ships were the 550-ton *Elizabeth Bonaventure*, which would serve as Drake's flagship; the *Golden Lion*, with William Borough, Controller of the Navy, as vice-admiral; the *Dreadnought*, commanded by Thomas Venner; and the *Rainbow*, captained by Henry Bellingham. Another four ships, including two of the Queen's pinnaces were appointed to the fleet as 'hand-maids'. Also, four ships were contributed by Drake, two by Lord Admiral Howard, one by John Hawkins, one by William Wynter, and another seven were provided by the Levant Company (which traded with the eastern Mediterranean).

On April 2, 1587, the fleet with its 2200 men, sailed for Spain. Drake was in high spirits, as evidenced by a letter he sent to Burghley: 'I find no man, but as all members of one body, to stand for our gracious Queen and country against Anti-Christ and his members... If your honour did now see the fleet under sail, and knew with what resolution men's minds do enter into this action, so you would judge a small force would not divide them... The wind commands me away. Our ship is under sail, God grant we may so live in His fear, as the enemy may have cause to say that God doth fight for her Majesty as well abroad as at home, and give her long and happy life and ever victory against God's enemies and her Majesty's.' 'At home' was a reference to the execution of Mary Queen of Scots and the rounding up of Jesuit priests.[4]

Drake's brief was 'to impeach the joining together of the King of Spain's fleet out of their several ports, to keep victuals from them, to follow them in case they should come forward towards England or Ireland, and to cut off as many of them as he (Drake) could and impeach their landing, and also to set upon such as should either come out of the West or East Indies into Spain, or go out of Spain thither'.[5]

However the Queen, who had given Drake her blessing, suddenly changed her mind, and countermanded her previous instructions. Drake was 'to forbear to enter forcibly into any of the said King's ports or havens, or to offer violence to any of his towns or shipping within harbouring, or to do any act of hostility upon the land'.[6] However, the vessel dispatched to give Drake his new orders failed to catch the fleet, and Drake sailed on.

On April 16, they encountered two ships enroute from Cadiz to 'Middleborough' (Middlesborough on the north-east coast of England), from whom they learnt that 'a great store of warlike provision', was being made at Cadiz.[7]

Vice admiral William Borough disapproved of the way Drake operated, and objected strongly when his commander summoned his captains, himself included, aboard his flagship for a council of war. Instead of holding a debate with them in the time-honoured tradition, he simply gave the order that they would proceed to Cadiz 'with al speed possible'.

Somehow, on April 27, Drake found time to write to his friend, the Reverend John Foxe (author of the history of the Protestant Martyrs), from the *Elizabeth Bonaventure*, and his letter gives an insight into the intensely religious nature of his character. He first says that he hopes that Foxe has remembered him and his colleagues in his prayers; and hopes that by his (Drake's) service to his country, 'God may be glorified, His Church our Queen and Country preserved', and 'the Ennymies of the truth... vanquished'.[8]

The information from the ships proved to be correct, for Lisbon and Cadiz were indeed the two principal ports of assembly for the Spanish Armada, of which the great galleons of Portugal would form the core, the remainder to be largely made up of newly-built or adapted merchantmen. Having arrived at Cadiz on April 24, Drake, anxious to bring the Spanish fleet to action, sent word to Santa Cruz, Spain's Lord High Admiral, in his typically jocular way, 'that hee (Drake) was there ready to exchange certaine bullets with him'. The Marquis, however, declined the challenge, whereupon Drake entered the harbour, where he was immediately 'assailed... by sixe Gallies', which then withdrew to the protection of the guns of the fortress. Here they discovered '60 ships and divers other vessels', of which 20 French ships fled to Port Real in the adjoining river estuary. Some Spanish vessels of small draught which could negotiate the shoals also fled.

The 1000 ton *Raguza* was immediately sunk with shot, after which four galleys attempted to engage, 'but altogether in vaine'. Before nightfall, 30 of the ships were in Drake's possession, including one of 'extraordinary hugeness belonging to the Marquesse of Santa Cruz'. It was Santa Cruz, (who had defeated the French fleet at Terciera in the Azores in 1583), whose idea it had been to send an army of invasion direct from Spain to Southern England; but because Philip could not raise the money, the plan was modified. Instead, before invading England, the fleet would first sail to the Netherlands to take on board the Spanish army serving there.

Among the vessels which Drake set fire to and destroyed at Cadiz were five 'great ships of Biscay', of which four were, 'taking in the King's (Philip's) provision of victuals for the furnishing of his Fleet at Lisbon', and the fifth, of 'about 1000 tunnes in burthen', they found to be 'laden with iron-spikes, nailes, yron (iron) hoopes' and 'horse-shooes'.

A ship of 250 tons, which was 'laden with wines for the King's provision', Drake 'caried out to Sea', and 'there discharged the said wines' for his 'owne store'. Having unloaded biscuit from a captured flyboat, they set fire to it but took two others 'in our company to the Sea'. Ten other ships, 'laden with wine, raisins, figs, oiles, wheat, & such like' were fired, bringing the total 'burnt, suncke, and brought away with us' to '30 at the least, being about 1000 tunnes of shipping'.

'This strange and happy enterprize was atchieved in one day and two nights, to the great astonishment of the King of Spaine, which bred such a corrasive (corrosive) in the heart of the Marques off Santa Cruz... that he never enjoyed a good day after, but within fewe moneths, died of extreame griefe and sorrow'. According to the essayist Sir Francis Bacon, Drake referred to the episode at Cadiz as, 'the singeing of the King of Spain's beard'.[9]

Drake, in a letter to Walsingham, indicated that there was still much work to be done. 'There must be a beginning of any great matter,' he said, 'but the continuing unto the end until it be thoroughly finished yields the true glory... God make us thankful again and again that we have, although it be little, made a beginning upon the coast of Spain.' Yet at the same time he was certain that the enemy would now seek revenge, 'with all the devices and traps he could devise'. He acquainted Walsingham of Spain's mighty preparations for war, the like of which 'was never heard of or known'. 'Prepare in England strongly,' he advised, 'and most by sea. Stop him now, and stop him ever.'[10]

∽

They then set sail towards 'Cape Sacre' (Cape Sagres, a headland near Cape St Vincent, south-west Spain), and on the way there, intercepted, sunk and burned 'neere an hundred' ships, barks and caravels 'laden with hoopes, gally-oares, pipe staves, & other provisions of the king of Spaine, for the furnishing of his forces intended against England....' The pipe staves referred to were the curved pieces of wood which form the sides of a barrel, and the hoops the circular metal bands which bound them together. Drake's action would therefore deprive the Armada of the essential containers for its water, wine and foodstuffs, during the long weeks it would spend at sea. Nevertheless, courteous as ever, Drake, showing no vindictiveness towards his prisoners, 'delt favorably' with the men (captured from the ships), and 'set them on shoare'. He now 'spoiled and consumed' all the fishing boats in the vicinity, hoping in this way to put paid to the tunny-fishing industry which flourished in those parts.

Having landed at Cape Sagres, they assailed its castle and three other strongholds which they took 'some by force and some by surrender'. Again, Drake's vice admiral, William Borough, opposed the former's action; this time recording his objections in writing. 'I have found you always,' he said, 'so wedded to your own opinion and will, that you rather disliked and showed as that it were offensive unto you that any should give you advice in anything.' Drake was furious, and reacted by placing his vice admiral under arrest in his own ship, the *Golden Lion*. Whereupon the crew of the *Golden Lion* took matters into their own hands and set sail for home. She arrived at Dover on June 5, whereupon William Borough was straightaway imprisoned. Drake in the meantime had convened a court martial which sentenced Borough to death in his absence, for mutiny and desertion.

Drake's fleet now, 'with consent of the chiefe of his Company' (this contradicts Borough's view that Drake was highly autocratic), set sail for the Azores (800 miles west of Portugal), by which time an epidemic of plague had spread throughout the fleet. Then in a storm, many of the merchant ships detached themselves and sailed for home. Approaching the island of St Michael (San Miguel), they had the good fortune to encounter the Portuguese carrack, *San Felipe*, which was returning to Portugal from the East Indies laden with a cargo of china, velvets, silks, gold, silver, and negro slaves to the value of £100,000 or more. (This was an indication of the huge importance of the East India trade and led, twelve years later, to the formation of the East India Company.) Having commandeered the *San Felipe*, Drake, with his usual generosity of spirit, provided her crew with boats and victuals and sent them on their way. This was a highly significant event, because the carrack was the first 'that ever was taken comming foorth of the East Indies; which the Portugals tooke for an evil signe, because the ship bare (bore) the King's owne name'. It also meant that every man of the fleet might now be enabled 'to have a sufficient reward for his travel'. It was also a great morale booster, and proved that the strength of 'the Portugals... is nothing so great as heretofore hath been supposed'.

Drake's fleet duly arrived back in Plymouth on June 26, 1587. The investors, having spoken to the captains of the ships and been advised that some of the plunder was unaccounted for, complained but to no avail. However, the Queen, whose share of the spoils amounted to £45,000, gave the ships' crews an extra two months pay as a bonus, and Drake himself gave an extra six months pay to every man who had been present at the capture of the carrack.

According to Plymouth's Black Book, Drake by his action 'did greatlie annoye the kinge of Spaines fleete', but the 'spices and other commodities' which he brought back to England were to the 'great comforte of her majesty and her subjects'.

Drake's action prompted Lord Burghley to write a letter of apology to King Philip of Spain, saying that Drake had disobeyed Queen Elizabeth's orders and was now in disgrace, but the truth was that the Queen was overjoyed at Drake's 'haul', estimated in value at around 500,000 ducats.[11] Philip's patience was now at an end. The Queen's procrastinations would henceforth be to no avail. England, the rogue state, must now be severely dealt with.

Drake now turned his attention to William Borough, whom he charged with cowardice and desertion. Borough's defence was that, having been relieved of his post, he no longer had jurisdiction over his men who in deserting, had acted of their own accord. When the case collapsed, Borough himself went on the offensive by reminding the court how Drake had deserted John Hawkins at San Juan de Ulua, with the result that 100 men were left on the shore to be captured by the Spanish authorities. 'All which time (since the desertion),' said Borough, 'I stood ever in doubt of my life, and did expect daily when the admiral would have executed upon me his bloodthirty desire, as he did upon (Thomas) Doughty'. Meanwhile, the Queen was attempting to appease the Spanish representative (in the absence of the expelled ambassador Mendoza) by pretending that she was greatly offended by the actions of Sir Francis Drake.[12]

◦◦

The damage inflicted by Drake at Cadiz and Sagres not only gave England more time to prepare for the forthcoming onslaught, but it was also a morale-boosting success for English arms, at a time when all else was gloom and despondency. His success made him even more certain that the fight must be carried to the enemy. He trusted 'That the Lord of all strengths will put into Her Majesty and her people courage and boldness not to fear any invasion in her own country, but to seek God's enemies and Her Majesty's where they may be found... if a good peace be not forthwith concluded, then these great preparations of the Spaniard may be speedily prevented as much as in your Majesty lieth, by sending your forces to encounter them somewhat far off, and more near their own coast, which will be the better cheap for your Majesty and people and much dearer for the enemy'.[13] In this, Drake was supported by Lord Howard, who wrote 'The delay of Sir Francis Drake going out may breed much peril. It will be of no use to refer to the armistice if the King of Spain should succeed in landing troops in England, Scotland or Ireland'. Both men were aware of the prowess of the Duke of Parma as a military leader. Were his troops to gain a foothold on English soil, then the outcome would not be difficult to predict!

10

Confrontation Looms

In the spring of 1587, King Philip of Spain sent forth an order from the Escorial, his palace near Madrid, for the building of a great fleet, the cost of which would be in the region of 10 million ducats (or 2.5 million pounds). This the King would finance from the gold and silver, which flowed in a seemingly inexhaustible stream, from his Spanish colonies in the Indies.

Pope Sixtus V gave the Armada his blessing, and as was customary for all expeditions against 'Turkes & infidels', minted a 'Cruzado' (special coin marked with a cross), 'with most ample indulgences (favours) which were printed in great numbers'. The Pope's support was dependent on the King of Spain enjoying the 'conquered realm, as a vassal and tributarie... unto the sea (See) of Rome', and 'to this purpose', he 'profered a million of gold, the one halfe thereof to be paid in readie money, and the other halfe when the realme of England or any famous port thereof was subdued'. The Pope even went so far as to dispatch an Englishman, the Lancashire-born and Oxford-educated Cardinal William Allen, who had fled abroad at the beginning of Elizabeth's reign, to conduct 'the administration of all matters ecclesiasticall throughout England'.

The fleet of 130 ships or more, divided into 10 squadrons, was gathered together from all parts of Spain and her empire, and the names and complement of the various squadrons were as follows: Portugal (10 galleons), commanded by the Duke of Medina Sidonia, who was also 'captain general' of the entire fleet; Biscay (10 galleons) under second-in-command, the veteran General Juan Martinez de Recalde, the finest sailor in the fleet; Guipuzcoa (province of Biscay, 10 galleons) under General Miguel de Oquendo; Castile (14 ships), under General Diego Flores de Valdes (a squadron otherwise known as the 'Indies Guard', whose normal task was to escort the annual 'Treasure Fleet' on its journey back to Spain from the Americas, and whose commander had twenty years of experience in the West Indies trade). However, de Valdes, having been ordered by King Philip to advise on tactical matters, did not sail aboard its flagship the *San Cristobal*, but instead sailed with the Duke of Medina Sidonia aboard the *San Martin*); Andalusia (10 galleons and other vessels) under Pedro de Valdes, cousin of Diego; Italy and its Levant islands (10 ships) under General Martin de Bertendona; Urcas (23 hulks or supply ships) under General Juan Gomez de Medina (included here were the English merchantman *Charity* and the Scottish merchant-man *St Andrew*, both of which the Spanish had previously seized and confiscated); Galleasses (4) under Don Hugo de Moncada, (the galle-ass being a long, low-built ship propelled by oars and sails); and Galleys (4), under Captain Diego de Medrano, (the galley being like a galleass but smaller and lighter). There was also a squadron of tenders, caravels (small, light, fast vessels) and others numbering 22 in all, commanded by General Antonio Hurtado de Mendoza.

The Duke of Medina Sidonia.
Photo: Archivo Propiedad Duques Medina Sidonia, Sanlucar de Barrameda, Spain.

The Duke of Medina Sidonia, or to give him his full name, Don Alonso Perez de Guzman el Bueno, was a cousin of King Philip II, and had been appointed 'Captain General of the Ocean Sea' on the death of his prede-cessor, the Marques de Santa Cruz, (held to be the ablest officer in the Spanish navy), in February 1588. Sober-looking, and sporting a well-trimmed beard and moustache, the Duke wore a high white collar, but was otherwise attired in black. Around his chest hung the chain and insignia of Spain's highest order of chivalry, that of Knight of the Honourable Order of the Golden Fleece.

An aristocrat and a provincial governor, the Duke was aged only thirty-eight, but he looked old beyond his years. When King Philip had decided to annex Portugal, it was the Duke whom he had chosen to command his army of invasion, and now the Duke was accorded the rare distinction of commanding the forces of Spain at sea, having previously commanded them on land, (even though he had never before captained a fleet of ships, nor even witnessed a battle at sea!) Hence his distinct lack of enthusiasm about the prospect of fulfilling his present role. 'Sir, I have not health for the sea,' he told his King, 'for I know by the small experience that I have had afloat that I will soon become seasick and have many humours.' His flagship was the 1000 ton, 48 gun, *San Martin* of the Squadron of Portugal.[1]

There were 8252 sailors in the fleet, 2088 galley-slaves, 19,295 soldiers, noblemen volunteers who, together with their attendants, numbered almost 2000. There were also apothecaries, cooks, blacksmiths, carpenters, and divers persons whose task it would be to untangle anchor cables or plug any leaks caused by shot. Also present was Don Martin Alaccon, administrator and vicar-general of the Holy Inquisition in charge of 290 monks, priests, and familiars (servants). The cost of maintaining the entire naval and military forces commanded by Medina Sidonia and Parma was estimated to be 30,000 ducats per day.

This was a truly cosmopolitan fleet, containing five regiments of Spaniards, together with 'many olde and expert souldiers chosen out of the garisons of Sicilie, Naples and Terceira' and 'many bands also of Castilians and Portugals...'. It was not lawful for any man, 'under grievous penaltie, to cary any women of harlots in the Fleete...', but the women were not deterred, and 'hired certaine shippes, wherein they sailed after the Navie'. However, some of their hired ships were driven by storms onto the coast of France.

Impressive as the fleet looked, its ships had one great impediment which was soon to cost them dear. They were so 'encumbered with top-hamper' (i.e. top-heavy with men, provisions and equipment), that they could 'bear but little canvas', even with mild winds and smooth seas. They therefore lacked both speed and manoeuvrability.

The objective of the Armada (from the Spanish meaning 'Armed Force') had been laid down by Medina Sidonia in his sailing orders. It was 'to regain countries to the Church now oppressed by enemies of the true faith'.[2] England's Protestant Queen, Elizabeth, he regarded as a heretic; she must therefore be deposed and the country restored to Catholicism. This would be achieved in the following way.

Medina Sidonia would sail from Lisbon to Calais, there to rendezvous with Parma and his infantrymen. Then, with Parma in command of the entire expedition, the combined force would cross the Channel and Parma's army, augmented by 6000 more troops from the fleet, would disembark and march on London. Meanwhile, Medina Sidonia would capture and fortify the Isle of Wight and prevent any interference from the English or Dutch fleets. Again, there was a fatal flaw, for King Philip and his advisors seemed unaware that off the coast of the Netherlands, the Dutch fleet was lying in wait.

The Duke of Parma was under no such illusions. His infantrymen had been reduced as a fighting force from 30,000 to 17,000, as a result of sickness and other unspecified causes, possibly desertions. 'England now,' he said, 'was alert and ready for us', and although another 6000 men supplied by Medina Sidonia, would increase his force to 23,000 men, it was his opinion that even 50,000 would be too few. Parma also had grave doubts as to whether his small collection of flat-bottomed river boats and hoys was capable of making the rendezvous at Calais, let alone of crossing the Channel.

For Philip, this was very much a religious crusade, and on his orders every man who sailed with the Armada was first to attend a ceremony of mass and confession at Lisbon's Cathedral of Se Patriarcal. On that occasion the priest had blessed the great standard of Captain General the Duke of Medina Sidonia, on which was emblazoned the red cross of Saint Andrew on a snow-white field, and the inspiring words, *Exurge Domine, et vindica causam tuum* ('Arise, O Lord, and vindicate Thy cause').

King Philip had ordered his squadrons not to break their battle formations, 'and that the captains, moved by greed', must not 'pursue the enemy and take prizes'. The quantity of food to be consumed by the men was laid down to the nearest ounce, and the sailing orders contained equal strictures regarding their moral behaviour. 'I call you one and all to abstain from profane oaths dishonouring the names of our Lord, our Lady, and the Saints... Each morning at sunrise the ships' boys, according to custom, will sing 'Buenos Dios' (good morrow) at the foot of the mainmast, and at sunset the Ave Maria...'. Since bad weather was likely to disrupt communications, a watchword was laid down for each day of the week: 'for Sunday, Jesus, and for the succeeding days Holy Ghost, Most Holy Trinity, St James, The Angels, All Saints, and Our Lady'.

Any misbehaviour or blasphemy aboard the ships would invite 'very severe punishment to be inflicted at our discretion'. No less than 170 priests and friars would sail with the fleet, to be on hand to take the services and absolve dying men of their sins, should the need arise.

Since the success of Drake's exploits at Cadiz, the Pope had regarded the Armada as a futile exercise. Describing King Philip as 'a poor creature', it was his opinion that 'the Queen of England's distaff (cleft stick used for spinning by hand) was worth more than Philip's sword', and that he would have preferred Elizabeth to embrace the Catholic religion, and thereby save herself from the impending danger.

SIR FRANCIS WALSINGHAM.

During the latter part of 1587, Elizabeth's spymaster's agents in Spain kept him informed of every detail of the preparations that the Duke of Medina Sidonia and his admirals were making. Sir Francis Walsingham knew the type of vessels being used, and how many men were to sail in them, and he possessed full inventories of the number of horses and amount of armour, ammunition and food which had been ordered. The Queen, however, was slow to heed Walsingham's warnings. So much so that on November 12, 1587 Walsingham wrote to Robert Dudley, 'the manner of our cold and careless proceeding here in this time of peril maketh me to take no comfort of my recovery of health, for that I see, unless it shall please God in mercy and miraculously to preserve us, we cannot long stand'.[3]

LORD HOWARD.

It was in the December of the previous year that the fifty-three-year-old Charles, 2nd Lord Howard of Effingham, Lord Admiral and cousin to the Queen, had been appointed 'lieutenant general and commander-in-chief of the navy and army prepared to the seas against Spain'. He had previously served as Member of Parliament for Surrey, and under the Earl of Warwick, as general of horse in the supression of the northern Catholic rebellion of 1569. In 1574 he was made Lord Chamberlain of the Household.

Sir Francis Drake, now in his mid-forties, was appointed his vice admiral, and there has been speculation as to why Drake himself was not given overall command. This, however, would have been impossible; the post having traditionally been filled exclusively by noblemen and officers of state. As for Sir Walter Raleigh, no post in the Royal Navy was offered to him, and instead he served as a member of a council of war engaged in drawing up plans for the defence of the realm. Finally, Raleigh's enthusiasm was rewarded and he did see action at sea against the Spaniards, albeit only in a minor role.

Unlike most of the Howard family who were Catholics, Charles was a Protestant. Thorough in his work, it was his boast that he had been aboard every ship that 'goeth out' with him. He had not previously participated in a naval battle, but in his favour was the fact that his father, Lord William Howard (who had trained him for his present position), and two of his uncles had been Lord High Admirals before him.

Charles, Lord Howard of Effingham, artist unknown.
Photo: National Portrait Gallery, London.

On a happier occasion, Lord Howard's father, Lord Admiral William Howard, great uncle to Queen Elizabeth and presently a Privy Councillor, had, with a fleet of 28 ships, escorted King Philip up the Channel for his marriage to Mary Tudor in Winchester Cathedral. When on that occasion the commanding Spanish admiral failed to haul down his colours, Lord William was obliged to fire off some rounds of shot to persuade him to do so, before according him an official greeting. Drake, the vice admiral, although vastly more experienced at sea, accepted Howard's appointment with good grace, and attended church with the Lord Admiral on Whit Sunday, praying and taking communion with him.

Lord Howard's flagship was the 800 ton, 55 gun *Ark*, which had previously been owned by and borne the name of Sir Walter Raleigh, who

119

had sold the vessel to the Crown.

The strategy had been for Howard, with 18 of the Queen's ships, to protect the English Channel, with Sir Francis Drake, operating from Plymouth in the 500 ton, 43 gun, *Revenge* (one of whose officers was Drake's first wife Mary's nephew, Jonas Bodenham, who was also his secretary and receiver or purser), in command of 36 armed ships, including seven of the Queen's galleons and 29 armed merchantmen. As soon as the ships had been assigned to him, Drake's first act was to deliver them to his cousin William Hawkins for a refit.

In the spring of 1588, Drake was anxious to make another pre-emptive strike against Spain, but no permission for this was forthcoming from the Privy Council, even though he had the full backing of Lord Howard, of his kinsman John Hawkins, and of Captain Martin Frobisher. Drake's strategy is summed up in a letter he wrote to the Privy Council: the fleet of Spain must by any means possible be stopped 'that they maye not come throughe the seas, as conquerors...'.[4] In other words, it was Drake's opinion that the fight should be taken to the enemy well before it could enter the English Channel. Drake was also anxious that his forces be strengthened, primarily to enable them to strike the first blow, and secondly because this would 'putt greate and goode hartes (heart) into her Majesties loving subjects, bothe abroade and at home...'.[5] Lord Howard, equally frustrated by the inactivity, even went so far as to express his regret to Sir Francis Walsingham. 'I am sorry,' he wrote '(that) her Majesty is so careless of this most dangerous time. I fear me much and with grief I think it, that her Majesty relieth upon a hope that will deceive her, and then it will not be her money nor her jewels that will help, for as they will do good in time so they will help nothing for the redeeming of time being lost.'[6]

As if his message had not been blunt enough, Drake spelled it out even more bluntly. With 50 'saile of shippinge', he told their Lordships, 'we shall doe more good upon their owne Coaste (i.e. the coast of Spain), then (than) a greate manye more (English ships) will doe here at home, and the sooner we are gone, the better we shal be able to ympeache (impeach) them'.[7]

There was another reason why it was of paramount importance for the Royal Navy to halt the Spaniards before they could set foot on English soil. England had no standing army, and relied for its defence upon the raising of military levies (forced conscription). As Henry Hastings, Earl of Huntingdon, so aptly put it, 'The soldiers are very rawly furnished, some lacking a headpiece, some a sword, some with one thing or another that is evil, unfit, or unbeseeming about him. They would sooner kill one another, than annoy the enemy'.

This so-called army would clearly be no match for the illustrious Duke of Parma. It was also recognised, that for the Spaniards to land, they would require a deep water anchorage, and therefore to frustrate them in this, a series of artillery forts were established at all such potential landing sites along the coast. Also, a large army was massed at Tilbury, on the River Thames, and fortifications erected on both sides of the river to resist any Spanish attack on London.

Drake now advised their lordships of another development, about which he had already forewarned them. A bark, which he had sent out to spy on the Spaniards, had returned with the news that 'Biskaines' (ships of the squadron of Biscay) were 'abroade' off the Spanish coast; not only that, but the Spaniards had the presumption to fly the English flags, with the 'redde Crosse'. This was not an attempt to mislead the English, which bearing in mind the enormous size of the Spanish fleet would have been preposterous, but in Drake's view, it demonstrated the enemy's haughtiness and pride, which would not be tolerated 'by any true naturall Englishe harte (heart)'.[8]

Lord Howard was a person of great humility who acknowledged and gave credit to the immense experience of his vice admiral, and the other sea captains, and was quite content to allow Drake to communicate freely, not only with the Privy Council, but also with the Queen herself. The latter took full advantage. He went on to point out his grave concern over the pitiful state of the fleet's ordinance. The powder and shot which Her Majesty's ships had been provided with was, in his opinion, so paltry as to be sufficient for a mere 'one daie (day) and halfes (half's) servyce'. He beseeched their lordships to 'consider deeplie of this', for it 'importeth but the losse of all'.[9]

A compromise was reached. Drake would take half his fleet to attack the Spaniards in the port of Lisbon, but leave the rest at Plymouth. By now however, he appears to have changed his tactics, for in a letter to the Queen, dated April 13, 1588, he talks of 'our intellengencs (intelligence)' being as yet uncertain, as was the resolution of his soldiers (which he would know better once they were at sea). In his mind was the previous flight of Captain William Borough in the *Golden Lion* after the raid on Cadiz. Another episode such as that would 'put the wholle (enterprise) in peril'.[10] However, Drake reassures the Queen that he has not in his lifetime known 'better men, and possessed with gall(anter) minds then (than) your majesties people are for the most part'.

The report from the bark of there being 300 ships assembled at Lisbon had given Drake pause for thought. Although this may well have been roughly the correct number, many of these vessels may have been supply ships, as the final strength of the Armada was to be 130 or so all told. Nevertheless, Drake realised that his was far too small a force to combat such a fleet. However, if the Queen would agree to strengthen his own fleet, and to provide sufficient 'victuall' for it to 'live withal uppon that cost (coast)', then he would be in a better position to fight, and to hinder the enemy's quiet passage to England.

Drake now made a profound statement which was to echo in military circles down through the ages. 'The advantage of time and place in all martial actions is half a victory, which being lost is irrecoverable... I most humbly beseech your excellent Majesty to have such consideration as the weightiness of the cause requireth...'. He described the 'present want (deficiency) of victuals', for the sake of which 'the whole service and honour' might be lost 'for the sparing of a few crowns'.[11]

Finally, after these repeated onslaughts by Drake, the Queen and her Council showed that they were alive to the situation by commanding Lord Howard to bring his fleet from Queensborough (Isle of Sheppey), where it had been guarding the mouth of the River Thames, to join forces with Drake's western fleet. However, Howard left 40 ships under the command of Lord Henry Seymour to patrol the English coast. When on May 23, 1588, Howard reached Plymouth, Drake took his ships out of harbour and formed a guard of honour to greet him.

కోం

The English fleet consisted of the following: 34 ships, 'great and small', and crewed by 6705 men, were provided by the Queen, of which the largest was the 1100 ton *Triumph*, and the smallest the 30 ton *Cygnet*; 32 merchant ships were appointed to serve under Sir Francis Drake; 30 ships and barks were provided by the City of London; 33 merchant ships and barks and 20 coasters, paid for by Her Majesty, served under Lord Admiral Howard; 23 coasters, paid for partly by Her Majesty but mainly by the 'Port Towns' served under Sir Henry Seymour; and 23 'voluntary ships that came into the fleet after the coming of the Spanish forces upon our coast...' were financed by Her Majesty 'for the time they served'.[12] Drake himself provided the 200 ton, 80 gun *Thomas Drake*, named after his brother and commanded by Henry Spindelow; this was one of many merchant vessels called into action. Drake's kinsman John Hawkins, commanded the 800 ton, 42 gun *Victory*, and Thomas Howard, cousin of the Lord Admiral, the 500 ton, 38 gun *Golden Lion*. The total was 197 ships and 15,925 men.

The ships of Lord Howard's fleet were, inadequately victualled. 'I know not,' said Lord Howard, 'which way to deal with the mariners, to make them rest contented with sour beer',[13] though in his opinion, he commanded 'the gallantest company of captains, soldiers and mariners that I think were ever seen in England.' An added problem was that his men were now falling sick in droves, and having to be replaced by less experienced hands. For Drake, however, the Lord Admiral had nothing but praise: '... how lovingly and kindly Sir Francis Drake beareth himself' he wrote to Walsingham 'and how dutifully to Her Majesty's service and unto me...'.

On July 29, the fleet set sail from Plymouth in favourable winds, only to be blown back there by a gale. However, scouting pinnaces reported the presence of enemy ships off the Isles of Scilly. These vessels, ignorant of the bulk of the Armada's retreat to Corunna, had sailed on to make the original rendezvous which had been decided upon before the fleet had left Lisbon. After almost a week, these vessels were located and recalled.

Lord Howard had hoped to intecept them, and to this end set sail again on August 2, only to be thwarted once more by adverse winds. The belief now was that the Armada had regrouped. He therefore decided to stay put and await its arrival.

Howard divided the English fleet, which now watched for the approach of the Spaniards, into three squadrons. He himself patrolled in mid-Channel, with Drake off Ushant and Hawkins off Scilly. Once again, however, bad weather drove it back into Plymouth.

Drake had been frustrated in his aim of taking the fight to the enemy. As the Spaniards approached, the question now was, could the situation be saved?

Under the presidency of Vice-Chamberlain Sir Francis Knollys (brother-in-law of Robert Dudley), a commission was appointed in March, 1588, whose members included Arthur, Lord Grey de Wilton, Sir John Norris and Sir Francis Drake (as the only non-army officer), to draw up plans for the defence of the realm.

୧୨

In his letters to the Queen and her Council, Drake revealed his quality and genius as a planner and strategist. Realising the importance of intelligence, and having sent a bark to reconnoitre, he knew the strength of the enemy's fleet being assembled at Lisbon (though the estimate of 300 ships was erronieous in that it was double the real number). He adjusted his tactics accordingly by requesting politely, but firmly, that his own fleet be strengthened. Also, knowing that supplies of powder and shot were woefully inadequate, he tried (but with only limited success) to extract more from the authorities.

11

The Armada Sets Sail

On May 28, 29 and 30, 1588, the Armada had set sail from Lisbon, leaving the safety of the River Tagus for the vast Atlantic Ocean. The elements, however were unkind, and three weeks later, when the fleet lay off Cape Finisterre, it was scattered by a storm.

Most vulnerable were the four galleys, with their high forecastles and sterncastles, and their low freeboard. Of these, the *Diana* sank with all hands, and so aware of the danger was the master of the *Vasana* that he resorted to desperate measures. The master sought the advice of one David Gwynn, a Welshman who had been captured and had spent the last eleven years in fetters as a galley-slave. The upshot was that Gwynn, by a ruse, was able to seize his chance, stab the master to death and, with his fellow slaves, overpower and kill the crew. Not only that, he also overpowered another of the galleys, the *Royal*, and sailed them both to the French port of Bayonne and freedom.

Only the fourth galley, the *Princess*, was able to rejoin the fleet, which had been forced to seek shelter in the port of Corunna; there to repair damage to the ships, and recruit new crew to replace those incapacitated by an attack of dysentery which had swept through the fleet.

So great was the damage to the hospital ship *Casa de Paz Grande* (one of two), that she had to be left behind. Likewise four other vessels, including the *David*, 450 tons, which was to have carried pack and draught animals (for carrying and hauling respectively).

It was not until July 22 that the fleet left Corunna, and by July 29 it lay off Lizard Point, the southernmost tip of Cornwall, giving the Spaniards their first sight of England. The *Santa Ana's* structure had become so strained that she began leaking. Her commander, Admiral Recalde, managed to transfer himself to the galleon *San Juan de Portugal* (vice-flagship of the Squadron of Portugal), and the *Santa Ana* was forced to put in to the French port of Le Havre. She took no further part in the action.

∽

English Ships and the Spanish Armada, 1588. English School, c.sixteenth century
Photo: © National Maritime Museum, London.

By the smoke, which began to appear from beacons lit on the hilltops along the English coast, the Spaniards knew that their presence had been noted, and on their ships, prayers were said for the success of the great enterprise on which they were embarked.

Lord Howard was now faced with a proposal from the Queen's Council which he found both astonishing and ludicrous. Walsingham told him that his plan to sail to the 'Isles of Bayona (off Vigo Bay), was 'not convenient'. Instead, he should 'ply up and down in some indifferent place between the coast of Spain and this realm...'. For Howard, who lacked victuals for his men, many of whom had succumbed to an outbreak of sickness in the fleet, this was nonsensical. There were also tactical considerations, which he made clear to the Council in his reply.

Howard had debated at length with Drake, Hawkins, Frobisher and Captain Thomas Fenner of the *Nonpareil*, men 'which I think the world doth judge to be... of the greatest experience that this realm hath'. Were he to position himself in such a place as to prevent an attack on Ireland or Scotland, and still have the 'weather gauge' (be to windward of the enemy), then he would be 'clean out of the way' (i.e. in the wrong place), should the Spaniards decide to attack England instead.

12
Enemy in Sight

L egend has it that when news of the Armada's first sighting off Lizard Point broke, Francis Drake – 'El Dragon' (the Dragon), as he was known to the Spaniards – was playing a game of bowls with Lord Admiral Howard and the other admirals and captains on the green sward of Plymouth Hoe (the grassy promontory overlooking the harbour), and that his reaction was, 'There's plenty of time to win this game, and to thrash the Spaniards too!'.[1]

However, the truth was that for the Lord Admiral the Spanish Armada could not have arrived at a worse time. Effectively trapped by wind and tide in Plymouth harbour, Howard had no alternative but to begin 'warping' his ships out, a process whereby a rowing boat went ahead of each vessel and laboriously hauled it forward on its anchor cable. The manoeuvre was successful, and at 3p.m. on July 30, the opposing fleets sighted each other through the mist and drizzling rain.

The Armada, in sight, from the picture by John Seymour Lucas, R.A., R.I.
Photo: City of Plymouth Museums and Art Gallery.

The Armada sailed in the form of a crescent, whose horns were separated by a distance of 7 miles. However, it was the English who had the advantage (the so-called 'weather gauge'), for they now lay to the west of the enemy and therefore to windward. Lord Howard commanded the 800 ton, 55 gun *Ark*, Drake his vice admiral the 500 ton, 43 gun *Revenge*, Hawkins as rear admiral and third-in-command the 800 ton, 42 gun *Victory*, and the famous sailor and explorer Martin Frobisher, the 1100 ton, 42 gun *Triumph*.

Medina Sidonia hoisted the royal standard, a signal for battle, but the English refused all offers of engagement and were content to attack only the rearguard, commanded by Recalde. The running skirmishes continued up Channel, until they were in sight of Plymouth, and all the time the English were being replenished and reinforced from the shore. As Plymouth's clerk recorded in his Black Book (ledger), under the auspices of John Hawkins' brother William, who was currently serving as the town's mayor, 'the enemyes came in open sight of our harborough (harbour)'.

On July 31, for the Spaniards, there came a self-inflicted blow. On board Admiral Oquendo's flagship *San Salvador*, a 958 ton, 25 gun vessel of the Squadron of Guipuzcoa, an enraged master-gunner who had been reprimanded for carelessness, deliberately laid a train to the powder magazine, fired it, and jumped overboard. The damage was immense; nearly 200 men were killed instantly, and about half the treasure was lost. This ship had been carrying the paymaster general of the fleet, and its war chest contained 55,000 gold 'escudos'. All Medina Sidonia could do was to send small vessels to rescue the remainder of her crew.

Finally, two galleasses arrived to tow the *San Salvador* in amongst the hulks to safety, which they did despite the efforts of the English to prevent them. The galleass was a vessel of about 600 tons with square-rigged foremasts and mainmasts and a lateen-rigged mizzen mast with banks of rowers (slaves, as in the galleys) on either side. A pointed iron tip on the bow served as a battering ram, and the largest gun on a galleass could fire a projectile weighing 50lbs. Speedy and manoeuvrable, these vessels were ideal for close-quarter skirmishes in a Mediterranean setting. However, out in the great oceans, their usefulness was limited.

The English hope was to isolate and cripple the ships of the Spanish rearguard but, as Drake commented dryly, 'As farre as we perceive, they (the enemy) are determined to sell their lives with blowes'.[2]

'The Surrender', by John Seymour Lucas, R.A., R.I.
Photo: City of Plymouth Museums and Art Gallery.

On the same day, Don Pedro de Valdes's flagship, the *Nuestra Senora del Rosario*, sustained damage to her foremast and mainmast in a collision with at least two other ships, and as night fell, was left behind by her compatriots. She fired her distress flares but on this occasion Medina Sidonia, for reasons best known to himself, did not attempt a rescue. The *Rosario* managed to fight off assaults by Frobisher and Hawkins, but the following morning she surrendered to Drake's *Revenge*.

She was a prize indeed, for newly built at Ribadeo in Galicia, at a cost of 22,000 ducats, the *Rosario* was the fourth largest ship in the fleet at 1150 tons and with 46 guns and a complement in excess of 440 men. De Valdes was brought aboard *Revenge*, along with about 40 Spanish officers and gentlemen who were duly made prisoner. Historian Emmanuel van Meteran states that 'Valdes comming unto Drake and humbly kissing his hand protested unto him, that he and his had resolved to die in batell, had they not by good fortune fallen into his power, whom they knew to be right curteous and gentle, and whom they had heard by generall report to bee most favourable unto his vanquished foe...'. Having heard this, 'Drake embraced him and gave him very honourable entertainment, feeding him at his owne table, and lodging him in his cabin'.[3]

Hawkins and Frobisher were hardly delighted with Drake, who had snatched what they hoped would be their prize from under their noses. So how had this come about when, the night before the surrender, Drake had been leading the fleet, using his stern lantern as a beacon? The explanation would not come until August, when Matthew Starke, sailor aboard Drake's *Revenge*, described how Drake and his crew had sighted four hulks, which they decided to pursue, 'not knowing what they were'. This was accepted by Lord Howard, but Frobisher was to complain bitterly that 'He (Drake) thinketh to cozen (defraud) us of our shares of 15,000 ducats...' and unless they (he and Hawkins) were given their shares, he Frobisher would make Drake 'spend the best blood in his belly'.[4]

The *Rosario* was then towed first to Torbay, and then to the more secure harbour of Dartmouth. The remainder of her company, soldiers and mariners who numbered 397, were now placed under the jurisdiction of Sir John Gilbert and George Cary, deputy lieutenants of Devon, and subsequently incarcerated in the tithe barn of Torre Abbey at Torquay. However Pedro de Valdes and a few others remained aboard Drake's *Revenge*. Finally, the *Rosario*, being an armed merchantman rather than a warship, was put to use by the English as a supply vessel.

There was silver plate aboard the *Rosario*, and chests containing in excess of 50,000 ducats. (However when Drake eventually handed the money over to the safe keeping of Lord Howard, the number had mysteriously diminished to only 25,300!) Another chest contained fine swords with jewelled hilts, which King Philip intended to present to sympathetic English Catholic peers after the invasion. There were 50 pieces of ordnance, the heaviest being a demi-cannon weighing 5230lbs. The 88 barrels of gunpowder and the 1600 shot (cannonballs) were dispatched immediately, to be gratefully seized upon by the English fleet.

Further light was shed on the fate of the *Rosario's* prize money when, shortly after the Armada campaign, Lord Howard commissioned Robert Adams, surveyor of the Queen's buildings, to produce a series of representations of the events that had taken place. One of these, reproduced by John Pine, London's finest heraldic and decorative engraver, depicted Sir Francis Drake 'distributing amongst his officers and soldiers, the money etc. that was found in a great Galleon brought into Dartmouth'.[5] Historian Richard Hakluyt later confirmed that the English soldiers 'merrily shared amongst themselves' the Spanish ducats from the *Rosario*.⁹ Whether this was done with the authority of the Privy Council is not known, but in any event it does demonstrate that all ranks benefited from the Spanish prize, and not just Drake himself.

Drake's chancing upon the richly laden *Rosario* appears at first sight to be coincidental, and Frobisher may be forgiven for being extremely jealous of his vice admiral for the capture. Or is it possible that Drake was only too well aware of what he was doing? Knowing his penchant for thorough reconnaissance and intelligence gathering, the latter would seem to be the more probable.

The loss of the *Rosario* was a serious blow for the Spaniards. Now the plans of their commander, the Duke of Medina Sidonia, would surely be discovered, if they were not known to the English already, and the success of the entire enterprise on which they were embarked might well be jeopardised.

∽

On August 1, Don Alonso de Leyva was placed in temporary command of the rearguard, while Recalde completed repairs to the damaged *San Juan de Portugal*. De Leyva's instructions were to engage the enemy at close quarters, as grappling was the tactic at which the Spaniards were best suited. However, the English were not to be drawn. The *San Salvador* was deemed by the Spaniards to be beyond repair, and those of her company who remained able-bodied were taken off, including her captain, who himself was badly wounded. The 'King's money', needless to say, was also removed. Some, who had been burnt in the explosion, were presumably transferred to the hospital ship *San Pedro Mayor*, but 50 or so others, too ill to be moved, had to be left behind.

When the *San Salvador*, now drifting off Dorset's Chesil Bank and taking in water, signalled for help, Lord Howard sent his cousin,Lord Thomas Howard, in the 500 ton, 38 gun *Golden Lion*, and Captain Hawkins in *Victory*, to board her and take possession of her as his prize. First, however, they had to drive away the Spanish feluccas which had been sent to scuttle her.

An inspection revealed that the *San Salvador*'s deck had collapsed, her steerage had broken and her sterncastle was burnt out. Aboard there remained 50 or so 'poor creatures, burnt with powder into the most miserable sort'.⁷ Also 140 barrels of gunpowder, which the English were to find most useful. In fact it is likely that without this extra gunpowder the English fleet would have been virtually incapable of pursuing their offensive. A bark was sent to tow the ship into Weymouth and, to prevent her from sinking, the pumps were manned. More of her crew died en route, and others in Weymouth itself, until finally only 17 remained. Ten of these were Spaniards, of whom the only nobleman was Don Melchor de Pereda. There were also two Frenchmen, four Almains (Germans or Flemings) and one Almain woman. The Privy Council ordered that the survivors were to be imprisoned at Weymouth on a diet of bread and water until further notice.

Orders were subsequently received for the *San Salvador* to be taken to Portsmouth, it having been decreed that all non-Spanish prisoners were to be released. However, whilst crossing Dorset's Studland Bay she began to sink. A small boat from Studland rescued 33 of her crew. The remaining 23, which included the two Frenchmen and the four Almains, were drowned when she went to the bottom.[8] The fate of the Almain woman is not known, but her presence begs the question, were there other women aboard the Spanish ships? So two of Spain's mightiest and most prestigious ships had been lost in one day, not by enemy action but by wilful damage and misadventure. Nonetheless, England was still in imminent danger, for were the Spaniards to invade, she was ill-equipped to fight a land battle.

A sloop was dispatched to the Duke of Parma to agree the exact site of the proposed rendezvous, and to seek from him the help of pilots acquainted with the Flemish coast. 'In case of the slightest gale in the world,' said Medina Sidonia, repeating his misgivings about the lack of a suitable anchorage, 'I don't know how or where to shelter such large ships as ours.'

By 5a.m. on August 2, when the Armada lay between Dorset's Portland Bill and St Aldhelm's Head, a change in the wind direction to north-east suddenly gave the Spaniards the weather gauge. The English failed to regain it by getting between them and the shore, and as they tacked to go seaward, the Spaniards attacked. In an action that continued sporadically all through that day, the Spaniards once again failed to close with and board their opponents, who fired off most of their powder and shot, despite being replenished from the land. The Spaniards were in a similar predicament, Medina Sidonia sending daily to Parma for supplies of four, six, and ten pound balls. Nonetheless, no great damage was inflicted by either side. The English ships were also constantly supplied with water and revictualled. The Spaniards enjoyed no such privileges.

During the night of August 2/3, the 650 ton, 38 gun *El Gran Grifon*, flagship and protector of the Squadron of Hulks, commanded by Juan Gomez de Medina, fell astern of the fleet, whereupon the ever-opportunistic Sir Francis Drake and his squadron surrounded her and raked her with shot. It was left to Admiral Recalde in the *San Juan de Portugal* to mount a rescue attempt.

The English fleet was now divided into four squadrons, under Howard, Drake, Hawkins and Frobisher, with Lord Henry Seymour patrolling the Straits of Dover. On August 4, with both fleets off Dunnose, on the Isle of Wight, it was the turn of the English to be put in danger, when Frobisher attacked the hulk *Santana* and one of the galleons of Portugal, which having been damaged, were lagging behind the Armada. The Spanish rearguard responded by pouncing on Frobisher and his ships, and were only held off with difficulty. Now Howard, with five of his galleons, drove right into the centre of the Spaniards, his *Ark* coming within a few hundred yards of Medina Sidonia's *San Martin*. This was the most vigorous action so far, with the English ships having no difficulty in hitting the huge Spanish vessels which, for their part, fired from their lofty turrets over the heads of their opponents. Then, having enabled Frobisher to extricate himself, Howard gave the signal to retreat. Drake and Hawkins now brought some local knowedge to bear, as they attempted to drive the Spaniards onto the 'Owers', a shoal some 10 miles to the east of the Isle of Wight.

On August 5, in recognition of their gallantry in the action of the previous day, Howard summoned Frobisher, Hawkins, Roger Townsend, Lord Thomas Howard, Lord Edmund Sheffield, and George Beeston to the *Ark* to confer on them the honour of knighthood.

On August 6, the Armada arrived at the Calais roads, closely shadowed by the English. Howard sent word to Lord Henry Seymour for his squadron to join the main fleet.

13

A Decisive Engagement

The Armada was now well within range of the Calais shore batteries, where Medina Sidonia found the Governor of Calais, Monsieur de Gourdon, well-disposed; so much so that he sent pinnaces with casks of water to replenish their supplies. By now the English had been reinforced, for Lord Howard had been joined by 36 ships of the so-called Squadron of the Narrow Seas (between England and the continent), commanded by Lord Henry Seymour in *Rainbow*, and including the veteran Sir William Wynter in *Vanguard*.

The inventor of the 'fireship' was the Italian engineer, Federigo Gianibelli, who was currently in London helping to construct fortifications on the River Thames. Combustible material would be loaded onto a vessel, which would then be fired and steered towards an anchored enemy fleet. It was Wynter's opinion that such tactics would be ideal in the present circumstances. After a council of war held with his senior commanders on August 7, Wynter's plan was approved. The English were about to launch their most terrifying attack. Meanwhile, M. de Gourdon sent his nephew to Medina Sidonia's flagship with assurances that France would not intervene in the dispute with England.

For twenty-four hours, the Armada lay in the Calais roads, exposed to the weather which fortunately for them had thus far been clement, and its dangerous shoals, as it awaited the Duke of Parma. Nevertheless, the enemy still constituted a potent force, because although the ships in the opposing fleets were comparable in number, the majority of the English vessels were merchantmen, and the Spaniards possessed twice the tonnage, four times the number of guns, and three times the number of men.

At an hour past midnight on the night of August 7/8, six flaming vessels propelled by wind and tide bore down upon the Spaniards.

There had been no time to send to England for hulks, so Drake came to the rescue by sacrificing one of his own ships, the *Thomas Drake*, for the purpose. Likewise Hawkins, who donated his 150 ton *Bark Bond*, and others. These vessels were loaded with barrels of tar and bundles of sticks ('faggots'), and then, with their guns shotted (loaded), sails set, and rudders secured, they were appropriately positioned according to wind and tide, fired, and let loose.

There was panic amongst the Spaniards, who were only too well aware that practically every part of a sixteenth century wooden warship was flammable, not to mention the gunpowder aboard. They remembered a similar attack by the citizens of Antwerp against Parma four years previously. There was no time to weigh anchor, so cables were cut and, in their frantic efforts to escape one ship became entangled with another. Two ships were set on fire, and many were disabled, including Moncada's *San Lorenzo*, the Armada's largest and most magnificent vessel, which had lost her rudder and whose crew were attempting to row her to the safety of Calais harbour.

The water was too shallow for Howard to reach her in the *Ark*, so he sent a longboat, manned with 50 or 60 volunteers, in pursuit. The *Margaret and John* had the same notion, but ran aground. Nevertheless, she dispatched a pinnace, manned with musketeers.

The great galleass failed to enter the harbour and became stuck fast upon the bar, whereupon the English came alongside and demanded she surrender. In the ensuing skirmish, Moncada was killed by a musket shot to the head, by which time several other small English boats were arriving. Many of the *San Lorenzo's* soldiers, of whom there were 300, leaped into the sea. Most were drowned, although some did succeed in reaching the shore. Finally, the ship surrendered, and its 300 or more slaves were liberated.

A French vessel arrived on the scene with instructions from its officers from M. de Gourdon that neither the ship nor its ordnance was to be removed. However, when some of the Englishmen offended these officers by robbing them of their rings and jewels, the French batteries began firing on the English, who were compelled to withdraw.

The pinnaces returned safely to the fleet and Lord Howard continued his pursuit of the Spaniards. At about 10a.m., combat began off Gravelines, with the wind west-north-west, and the English now having the advantage of both tide and weather gauge.

Drake in *Revenge*, followed by Frobisher in *Triumph*, and Hawkins in *Victory*, led the attack on the Spanish flagships. In a battle which lasted six hours, the English prevented their foes from returning to their station off Calais, and also resisted their attempts to come alongside and grapple and board. In the words of Captain Winter, 'When the cartridges were all spent, and the munitions in some vessels gone altogether, we ceased fighting, but followed the enemy, who still kept away.'[2] 'We have chased them in fight,' said Lord Howard, 'until this evening late, and distressed them much; but their fleet consisteth of mighty ships and great strength... Their force is wonderful, great and strong, and yet we pluck their feathers by little and little.'[3] That 'one day's service had much appalled the enemy', observed Drake.[4] However, had the Spaniards known the true situation, that the English had run out of munitions, then this might have been the opportunity to counter attack. For the English, no ship was lost, and fewer than 100 men had been killed.[5]

The Spaniards had lost three of their great ships, whilst others having been disabled by English gunfire and by collisions with their compatriots, found themselves being driven by the wind ever nearer to the treacherous sandbanks of Holland. By late afternoon, the toll of Spain's best ships had reached 16, with many hundreds, if not thousands of men killed in action.

After the battle, Drake wrote to Secretary of State Walsingham: 'God hath given us so good a day in forcing the enemy so far to leeward as I hope in God the Prince of Parma and the Duke of Sidonia shall not shake hands this few days. And whensoever they shall meet, I believe neither of them will greatly rejoice of this days service.'[6]

Medina Sidonia had no choice but to give the order to retreat, and the remnants of the Armada now made for the open sea, leaving the remainder of its ships to their fate. Of these, the *San Mateo* was engaged by the Dutch Sea Beggars, to whom she surrendered after a two hour fight. The *San Felipe*, dismasted and drifting, was captured by the Dutch and escorted into Flushing, and *La Maria Juan* of the Squadron of Biscay went down with all hands. But what of the Duke of Parma?

Parma had always proposed that a port such as Flushing should be seized to use as a base for operations against England. Having been overruled on this point he at least expected that the Armada would clear the way for him before he set sail with his cosmopolitan force of Walloons (Belgians), Burgundians, Dutch, Germans, English, Scots,

Irish, and of course, Spaniards. He had gone to great lengths to improve the waterways between Spanish controlled Ghent and Sluys, Newport and Dunkirk, to which places he had transported all his hoys, barges and munitions, knowing that here they would be out of reach of the Hollanders and Zeelanders. Unfortunately for Parma, however, the fighting vessels of the Armada were of too deep a draught to negotiate such shallow waters.

On hearing on August 8 that the Armada had arrived at Calais, that same night Parma travelled to Newport and embarked with 16,000 men for Dunkirk, arriving there before dawn. He placed the troops stationed in that port aboard the transports, amongst them the English knight Sir William Stanley, with his 700 Irish foot soldiers. Now they waited patiently for the Armada to rid the coast of the watching Dutch fleet, whereupon thay expected to be given the order to set sail for England. However, it was not to be, for the Prince of Ascoli had come ashore from the Armada at Calais to bring word to Parma that following the fire-ship attack, the Armada had been put to flight. Drake was later to say of Parma, 'I take him to be as a bear robbed of her whelps'.[1]

Since the capture of the *Nuestra Senora del Rosario* by Drake, her captain, Pedro de Valdes and a handful of other prisoners had remained aboard his ship *Revenge*, giving them the unique if unenviable distinction of witnessing the conflict from the opposing side. Aware that his prisoners, especially Pedro de Valdes, would command a high ransom, Drake was naturally unwilling to let them out of his sight. On August 10 the prisoners were landed at the Sussex port of Rye, and taken to London by order of the Queen to be 'examined', but Pedro de Valdes, probably at Drake's request (to keep matters in the family, as it were), was placed in the charge of Drake's kinsman, Richard Drake of Esher, in Surrey.

To what could the English ascribe their victory over the mighty Armada? Good seamanship was certainly a factor, as was the greater manoeuvrability of the English ships, which made the Spanish vessels, with their towering forecastles and sterncastles, seem clumsy by comparison. However, it was in the field of gunnery where the English excelled.

The Weald (ancient forest) of Kent was the centre of a great iron industry, where, at a hundred or so sites, water wheels drove the blast furnaces which produced cast iron in huge quantities from local iron ore. This was used to mass produce cannon, which up until then had been made of bronze at great expense. The Spaniards, on the other hand, had no home industry, and were obliged to import their cannon from Italy, or from England on the black market.

The design of these cannon was also an important factor. The English ones were mounted on four-wheeled carriages which, having been fired, could then easily be hauled back inside the ship for reloading. The Spanish cannons however, had only two wheels and a long 'trail' (lower part of gun carriage), which meant that they were relatively immobile, and could only be reloaded by the expedient of climbing out along the barrel; an impossible feat when under fire in a rolling sea. Therefore, the English guns could fire at an immensely faster rate than their enemy.

Each bronze cannon on the Spanish ships was embossed with an escutchion (shield) depicting the arms of King Philip II of Spain and his former Queen, Mary Tudor of England. It was an irony that, had Mary lived, there would have been no conflict with England, and therefore no Armada.

As for tactics, the Spaniards, being more suited to skirmishes in the Mediterranean, hoped desperately that the English would approach near enough for them to do what they did best, namely grapple and board; for their forte was musketry and hand to hand fighting. The English would have none of it, and why should they when, with their superior guns, they could 'stand off' and fire from long range.

14

Flight

On the morning of August 9, the English fleet of 104 ships lay off the island of Walcheren, in the estuary of the River Scheldt in the Zeeland province of the Netherlands. The Armada lay to windward, and in the hope of bringing the enemy to battle, Medina Sidonia ordered his ships to lie in wait; but the English were not to be drawn. As the north-west wind freshened, the water beneath the keels of the Spanish ships grew shallower, as they were driven remorselessly towards the shoals of Zeeland, and in particular the Ooster Zand. However, just as it seemed that destruction was imminent, the wind veered to the south-west, enabling the Armada to sail once more for the open sea.

At 4p.m. Howard fired his signal gun and raised a flag to summon his commanders to a council of war. With Drake, Hawkins, Frobisher and Seymour in attendance, but not Winter who had been wounded, it was decided that Seymour and Winter should return to Margate to guard the mouth of the River Thames against any possible invasion attempt by Parma, and that the remainder of the fleet should continue the pursuit of the Armada.

From the night of August 9 until August 12, the pursuit continued, much to the delight of Drake. 'We have the army of Spain before us,' he wrote, 'and hope with the grace of God, to wrestle a pull (fall) with them. There was never any thing pleased me better than seeing the enemy flying with a southerly wind to the northward. God grant you have a good eye to the Duke of Parma, for with the grace of God, if we live, I doubt not so to handle the matter with the Duke of Sidonia as he shall wish himself at St Mary's Port (Cadiz) among his orange trees'.[1] However, there was to be no more 'wrestling', and on August 12, with the fleets at a latitude of 56°17', Howard and his council decided to put into Scotland's Firth of Forth to provision and replenish water supplies. Said Lord Howard, 'Notwithstanding that our powder and shot was well nigh spent, we put on a brag (boastful) countenance and gave them chase, as though we had wanted for nothing.'[2] The English now turned for home, 'leaving the Spanish fleet', as Drake put it in a letter to the Queen, 'so far to the northwards that they could neither recover England nor Scotland'.[3] Meanwhile two pinnaces were to 'dog the fleet (Armada) until it should be past the isles of Scotland'.[4]

On August 14 the wind changed to south-west, and in Howard's words, the ensuing storm was 'more violent... than was ever seen before at this time of the year'.[5] Now it was the turn of the English to be discomfited, as their fleet was scattered and many ships found themselves in danger of being driven onto the shoals off Norfolk. However, within a few days, all returned safely to Margate (north-east Kent).

For the Spaniards, immense hardships were to follow. A great storm blew for almost two days and nights. Provisions of bread, biscuit, cheese, bacon and fish soaked in vinegar were virtually exhausted, and so great were the shortages that rations were reduced to 8 ounces of biscuit, a small measure of water and a little wine per day. In an effort to conserve precious supplies of water, 40 fine horses and 40 mules, whose normal task was to haul the artillery pieces of the siege train, were herded unceremoniously over the side of the flagship *San Martin*. Those aboard the other ships did likewise. Men grew weak from starvation and dysentery, and there were many deaths, especially amongst the already weakened wounded, being cared for below decks on the hospital ship *San Pedro Mayor*.

The coasts of Norway and Scotland now claimed their victims, in a succession of storms which raged during the remainder of the month of August. It is doubtful whether there were charts to steer by, for no one had envisaged that the great fleet would find itself at these latitudes. The Spaniards, with some exceptions, were generally well treated by the Scots, where even among Scottish Protestants there was little animosity towards them, compared with that which prevailed in England and Ireland.

Want of water and provisions for their debilitated crews forced many ships to seek shelter and succour on the shores of Ireland, with results that were almost invariably disastrous. No less than 36 Spanish vessels were either overwhelmed by tempestuous seas or wrecked on the shores of Ireland, where the few Spaniards that survived were either swiftly butchered, or sent coupled in halters across country to be finally shipped to England. It was Sir Richard Bingham, Governor of Connaught, whose garrisons held the seaport towns on Ireland's west coast for

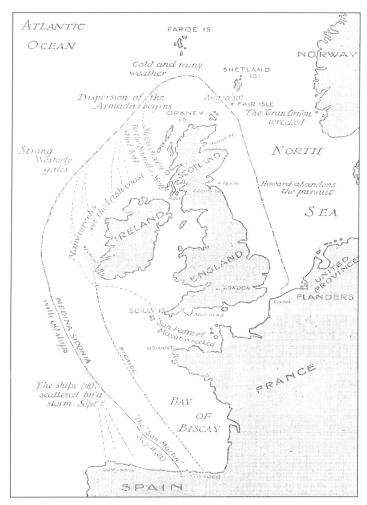

The Homeward Voyage of the Armada. © Thomas Nelson and Sons.

Queen Elizabeth's Lord Deputy in Ireland, Sir William Fitzwilliam. The ferocity of the English towards the Spaniards may be explained, though not excused, by the fact that Queen Elizabeth had a mere 6000 troops to garrison the whole of Ireland which, like Spain, was a Catholic country (but governed by Protestants) and therefore ripe for rebellion.

141

Salamander pendant of gold with rubies, from the wreck of the Girona.

Gold ring, depicting a hand enclosing a heart and inscribed with the prophetic words 'No tengo mas que dar te' (I have nothing more to give thee), from the Girona.

Of the 30,000 men who had sailed with the Armada, a mere one third were destined ever to see their native land again, and of the 130 vessels which originally embarked, only 53 returned to Spain. It was not until October that the Duke of Medina Sidonia reached Santander, giving King Philip false hope that 'the greater part of the Armada' was still intact.[6] He was soon to discover his mistake! Other Spanish ships went ashore near the French port of Rochelle.

Commanders Recalde, Oquendo and Bobadilla were either lost at sea, or died soon after their return. At an enquiry into the loss of Pedro de Valdes's flagship *Rosario*, Medina Sidonia was able to prove that it was on the advice of Flores de Valdes that he had abandoned the ship to her fate. For this reason, Flores de Valdes was sentenced to serve a period of fifteen months in prison.

The ships of the Armada had carried an estimated six million ducats (equivalent to one year's running costs for the entire fleet), virtually all of which was lost, and to make matters worse, the Pope refused to pay his promised one million ducats towards the venture.[7]

Summing matters up, Drake observed dryly that, 'Their invincible and dreadful navy, with all its great and terrible ostentation, did not in all their sailing about England so much as sink or take one ship, bark, pinnace, or cock-boat (ship's boat) of ours, or even burn so much as one sheep-cote (pen) on this land'.[8]

It was not only the Spaniards who were suffering. Since the latter days of August, men had been dying in the English fleet in their hundreds, or even thousands, of ship-fever (typhus). At Margate, they either died aboard ship, or in the streets of the town, in the absence of hospitals to admit them to. 'Tis a most pitiful sight,' said Howard, 'to see here at Margate how the men, having no place where they can be received, die in the streets. I am driven of force myself to come on land to see them bestowed in some lodgings; and the best I can get is barns and such outhouses, and the relief is small that I can provide for them here. He ends, 'It would grieve any man's heart to see men that have served so valiantly die so miserably.'[9] In fact so weakly manned were many of the ships that Lord Henry Seymour declared that there were not enough available mariners to weigh the anchors.[10]

Meanwhile, Sir Martin Frobisher was still angry with Drake for having captured the prize ship *Rosario*. According to Matthew Starke, mariner aboard Drake's flagship *Revenge*, Frobisher made a speech in front of Lord Edmund Sheffield (of the *White Bear*) and Sir John Hawkins. 'Sir Francis Drake reporteth that no man hath done any good service but he,' said Frobisher, 'but he shall well understand that others have done as good service as he, and better too. He came bragging up (boasting) at the first indeed, and gave them his prow (bow guns) and his broadside, and then kept his luff (maintained his course, sailing close to the wind), and was glad that he was gone again, like a cowardly knave or traitor – I rest doubtful which, but the one I will swear.' As regards the *Rosario*, Drake, like a coward, stayed with the ship all night, 'because he would have the spoil'. Drake 'thinketh to cozen us of our (his and Hawkins') shares of 15,000 ducats, but we will have our shares, or I will make him spend the best blood in his belly...'.[11] A subsequent inventory however, showed that in the action, Drake's *Revenge* had suffered more than most, with its mainmast 'perished with shot...'. There was damage to the rigging, and widespread 'pestering' (surface damage, rather than penetration) of its hull by cannon shot, showing that he had been in the thick of the action.

The Queen, anxious about the drain on her exchequer, was anxious to disband the fleet, but Drake urged caution. 'My poor opinion is,' he said, 'that I dare not advise her Majesty to hazard a kingdom with the saving

143

of so little charge.' The Duke of Parma was 'nigh', and would not 'let (omit) to send daily to the Duke of (Medina) Sidonia, if he may find him'.[12]

So great had been the cost of defending England that at the end of the Armada campaign, there were insufficient funds available to pay the mariners their 10 shillings per month, let alone to provide medical care for the sick and injured. The Queen had contributed what she could: since the year 1570 she had spent £9000 on timber and plank, had borne the cost of fitting out her Royal ships and building new ones, such as the medium sized galleon *Foresight*. She had also paid for the building of other ships, such as Sir William Wynter's *Edward* and *Mary Fortune*. In January, 1588, the Queen was obliged to raise £75,000 in loans from wealthy subjects, supplemented by a loan of £30,000 from the City of London, which charged interest at 10 per cent. Even this was not enough, and she was finally forced to borrow another £26,000 from the City. Beside this, Acts of Parliament were passed for collections of monies to be made throughout the parishes of the land. This prompted Lord Howard, who was not himself a wealthy man, to declare, in reference to providing funds out of his own pocket for the maintenance of the fleet, 'I will myself make satisfaction as well as I may, so that Her Majesty shall not be charged withal'.[13]

Within two years the 'Chatham Chest' naval charity was founded by the Queen, 'by the incitement, persuasion, approbation, and good liking of the lord admiral and of the principal officers of the navy', including Howard, Drake and Hawkins. Every serving seaman would donate each month a small proportion of his pay for the benefit of his fellow men wounded in action, and for that of the widows and orphans of those killed in naval battles. In 1592, this was taken further when, by Act of Parliament, every parish in England and Wales was 'charged to pay' a weekly sum of money towards 'hurt and maimed soldiers and mariners'. As far as is known, the original chest, made presumably of iron, no longer exists. (However, a Chatham Chest, ordered in 1625, is to be seen in the National Maritime Museum, London.)

৩৩

Now was the time for celebration, and with much pageantry and trumpeting, the Queen left her capital and journeyed on the royal barge from St James's (central London) to Tilbury, where Robert Dudley, Earl of Leicester had organised a parade of London's defensive forces for her inspection. Here Elizabeth, who arrived in a gilded coach escorted by 2000 troops, was to make her most memorable speech. 'My loving people... I come among you at this time but (not) for my recreation and pleasure, being resolved in the midst and heat of the battle to live and die amongst you all, to lay down for my God, and for my kingdom and for my people mine honour and my blood even in the dust. I know I have the body but of a weak and feeble woman, but I have the heart and stomach of a King, and of a King of England too – and take foul scorn that Parma or any Prince of Europe should dare to invade the borders of my realm...'.[14] In a 'Songe of Thanksgiving', which she herself composed, she gave thanks to the Almighty: 'He made the wynds and waters rise, To scatter all myne enemies...', she wrote.

❧

At the end of August, Admiral Justin of Nassau visited Dover with his fleet, dined with Seymour, and reported on the situation in the Netherlands. The Duke of Parma was unwilling to embark on any further enterprises against England, said Nassau, and in any case there were 25 Dutch ships ready and waiting 'to prevent his egress from Sluys'.[15]

Meanwhile, King Philip had not yet given up hope. On September 3, he suggested to Parma that this would be a good opportunity to set sail for England, while the English fleet was repairing its damage. ''Twill be easy enough for you to conquer that country,' said the King, 'as soon as you set foot on the soil. The perhaps our Armada can come back and station itself in the Thame (River Thames) to support you.'[16] On September 4, Dudley, once the Queen's favourite suitor, died of a fever at his home in Cornbury, Oxfordshire, aged fifty-six.

By September 15, Philip was under the impression that the Armada was sheltering and refitting in a Scottish port. 'In case the Armada is too shattered to come out,' he wrote to Parma, 'and winter compels it to stay in that port, you must cause another Armada to be constructed at Emden (on the coast of Holland) and the adjacent towns, at my expense, and, with the two together, you will certainly be able to conquer England.'[17] It was only when Medina Sidonia arrived at Santander that the King divested himself of his delusions.

One Armada vessel was to have the unique distinction of achieving what the Armada had failed to achieve and land in England, and on the shores of Sir Francis Drake's very own county, Devon.

Having become separated from the Armada fleet in the continual storms, she landed on September 28, 1588 at Ross (Ross Port, east of Erris Head, County Mayo), near to where they discovered the wreckage of another Armada ship, the *San Nicholas Prodaneli*. When ten men from the *San Pedro Mayor* set off in search of food, they were captured by English soldiers and joined their fellow countrymen from the *Prodaneli* in prison. These prisoners were executed, the English having refused an offer of ransom money from the Spaniards. The survivors did manage to find food, and set sail again on October 21, but when the *San Pedro Mayor* was a mere thirty leagues from the Spanish coast, the wind changed and drove the ship (which by now had lost her anchor) back up Channel.

She was finally blown ashore at midday on November 6, on the inhospitable rocks of Hope Cove, five miles west of Salcombe in South Devon, where the local fishermen, to their credit, brought out their boats to help the Spaniards ashore.

Owner of the greater part of the land between Hope Cove and Salcombe was Sir William Courtenay, a Catholic whose home was Ilton Castle, a fortified mansion near Salcombe. It was rumoured, that in the event of a successful invasion by the Spaniards, with whom he sympathised, Sir William hoped to regain the Earldom of Devonshire (this title having earlier become extinct when a previous earl died without issue) and his family seat, Powderham Castle, which was situated to the south of Exeter and overlooked the estuary of the River Exe.

158 men survived the wreckage of the *San Pedro Mayor*, out of the 180 who had originally sailed from Corunna, and others who had been transferred to the 'hospital' from other vessels of the fleet, having been burnt (in the explosion and fire aboard the *San Salvador*) or wounded. Various nationalities were represented, including Dutch, French, Italian, Portuguese, and of course Spanish.

The survivors were rounded up and imprisoned, probably in the bridewell (house of correction – the name deriving from such a place near St Bride's Well, in London) at Kingsbridge, where they joined 226 men from the captured *Rosario*, which had surrendered to Drake four months previously. (The remaining 166 men from the *Rosario*, owing to the expense of keeping them, were put back aboard the Spanish ship.)

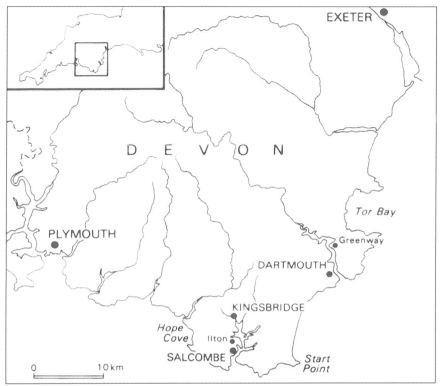

Map of South Devon   © University of Exeter Press.

The prisoners were provided for by George Cary, one of Devon's deputy lieutenants, at his own expense. The *San Pedro Mayor*, he affirmed, could not be recovered, as 'she lieth on a rock, and (is) full of water to her upper decks'.[18]

Now the Privy Council instructed that any men 'of quality and calling' amongst the prisoners were to be separated, with a view to their being sent to London and ransomed. As for the remaining 'soldiers and common people', all those who were 'Spaniards born' were to be executed, as 'most pernicious enemies to Her Majesty and the Realm'. This would include not only those from the *San Pedro Mayor* and *Rosario*, but also others from the *San Salvador*, and from the galleass *San Lorenzo* which had been sacked by the English when she ran aground beneath the walls of Calais Castle.[19]

147

15

Aftermath

In November, 1588, Drake and his wife Lady Elizabeth, who now spent much of their time in London, purchased the lease of a fine mansion called 'The Herbor'. Situated half a mile to the west of St Paul's Cathedral in the parish of St Mary Bothaw, it had a fine water frontage and gardens, and was once the royal residence of King Richard III. Drake had always craved respectability, ever since suffering the humiliation of being forced to leave his beloved home and County of Devon as a child. Now he had achieved it, at any rate in a material sense. Meanwhile, intelligence was received that ships of the Spanish Armada were beginning to arrive back in Spanish ports in significant numbers.

A fleet was therefore assembled, to be commanded jointly by Sir Francis Drake and Sir John Norris (a soldier who had fought with distinction in France, Ireland and the Netherlands), whose task was to repeat the previous success at Cadiz, by destroying Spanish ships in their home ports. However, a second and more contentious objective was proposed which was to install the pretender, Dom Antonio de Crato who was currently living in London, on the throne of Portugal; that country having been annexed by King Philip in 1580.

The Queen and Lord Burghley were not enamoured of this latter proposal, whose main proponents were Drake and the headstrong young Robert Devereux, 2nd Earl of Essex. Their vision was of an alliance with a liberated Portugal, which would provide the English with trade concessions in the East Indies, and a base in the Azores from which to attack the Spanish treasure ships. This notion prevailed; the Queen, Drake and Norris contributed the sum of £20,000 each to the enterprise.

The fleet, with Drake in his flagship *Revenge*, comprised six of the Queen's ships, two pinnaces, and 18 merchant vessels. There were also 60 or so Dutch fly-boats (long, narrow, swift sailing boats) which had been intercepted and pressed into use. The soldiers were reinforced by a contingent of veterans from the Netherlands campaign. Together with the seamen, the total complement was 23,375, with victuals sufficient for three months. After long delays caused by bad weather, it was not until April 28, 1589 that they finally sailed from Plymouth.

The twenty-three-year-old Essex defied the Queen, who had forbidden him to take part in the expedition, by stowing away aboard Sir Roger Williams's *Swiftsure*, flagship of a flotilla which had sailed from Falmouth, and joined Drake's main fleet near Bayona (near Vigo, northwest Spain). When news of this reached Elizabeth, she was most displeased. This was the first of several insubordinations by Essex, which resulted eventually, in the Queen's one-time favourite losing his head, literally!

For reasons best known to himself, Drake made no attempt to attack Santander and destroy the large number of Spanish ships which had gathered there. Instead, he sailed for Corunna where, on May 4, ships were burnt and the lower town plundered. However, an attack on the upper town was repulsed. They sailed on to the Portuguese town of Peniche. But by this time, men were dying in droves from typhus and dysentery. Here, troops led by Essex, defeated the local garrison after two days of fighting. The English soldiers then began to march the 45 miles southwards to Lisbon, the Portuguese capital. The city's Spanish garrison, however, had been forewarned by an informer in the company of Don Antonio, and resisted so effectively that the English were unable to breach the city's walls. They were further dismayed that, despite Dom Antonio's assurances, there was an almost total lack of support for him from his fellow Portuguese. In the retreat from Lisbon, many English wounded had to be abandoned to their fate.

Drake waited off Cascais, to the west of Lisbon, for Norris and his exhausted army to arrive, and in the meantime blew up its castle. Here, a large number of Spanish and neutral ships were captured. Sixty of these, which belonged to the Hansa (guild of German commercial cities) and were laden with corn and materials for the repair of the Armada ships, were added to the fleet; the Dutch fly-boats previously commandeered were allowed to sail for home. Then, on June 3, the decison was made to withdraw. As the fleet passed Peniche, ships were dispatched to fetch the small garrison of troops which, as a precaution, had been left there to defend the town in the event of Norris's army being forced to withdraw northwards. It was however too late. The Spaniards had massacred the garrison and its commander had fled.

Now the Queen, furious at this debacle, sent an angry despatch demanding at the very least, the capture of an island in the Azores. However, bad weather prevented this, and instead Drake sailed for Vigo, where he and Norris found nothing of value as, once again, its occupants had been forewarned of their approach. The town was fired and the troops returned to their ships for the journey home. These events were faithfully recorded in Plymouth's Black Book. Although Drake and Norris 'touke diurs (divers) places of Forces in Spaine', yet having 'a greate sicknes happeninge emongst theire men' they returned without 'entringe into the Cytie of lisborne (Lisbon), to which place theire chief bent was...'.

The Queen subsequently asked Drake and Norris 'to express her thanks to the colonels, captains, and inferior soldiers and mariners, who had shown as great valour as ever nation did'.[1] In truth, though, she was angry with her joint commanders for wasting this unique opportunity to destroy Spain's naval power. It would be another five years before she would give Drake another command.

Estimates vary as to how many English lives were lost, but the number was probably somewhere between 11,000 and 16,000 men. However, the destruction of shipping and stores which was achieved, effectively put an end to Spanish hopes of mounting another invasion attempt in the foreseeable future. As for Don Antonio, he spent the remainder of his days on the continent until his death in Paris.

So what of the fate of the prisoners from the wrecked Spanish hospital ship the *San Pedro Mayor*? Devon's deputy lieutenant Cary informed the Privy Council that he could find no men of any account amongst them. Eight, including her captain, the senior staff of the hospital, and two gentlemen adventurers were placed in the charge of Sir William Courtenay; Cary retaining two others in his own charge, namely the surgeon and the apothecary.[2]

On November 27, the Council ordered that the ten Flemings and ten Frenchmen amongst the prisoners be released, and by December 2, it rescinded its proposal that the Spanish-born prisoners be executed.

By December 28, the prisoners had become 'greatly diseased', and were therefore removed to various isolated barns and outhouses, in case 'the contagiousness of such sickness' infected other inhabitants in the vicinity.[3] By January, 1589, all the Portuguese prisoners from the Armada, including 13 from the *San Pedro Mayor*, had been released, on condition that they agreed to return to their native land with Drake and Norris's expedition.

The endless wrangling over what ransoms were to be paid for the Spanish prisoners dragged on from months into years, and involved Don Pedro de Valdes, who was himself still a prisoner. In a gesture of humanity, De Valdes requested that attention be given to the ransoming of the poor men first. When three of the *San Pedro Mayor's* prisoners viz. the captain, the surgeon, and the overseer of the hospital were paroled, all three managed to escape and were back in Spain by February, 1589.

On November 24, 1589, all remaining Spanish prisoners in England, including those from the *San Pedro Mayor*, were released by order of the Queen, except for 12 when she entrusted to Sir William Courtenay. They were treated harshly, as Gonzalo de Castillo, a gentleman adventurer from Granada recorded some years later. Sir William 'eftsoons straitly imprisoned us', he said, 'requiring from us 5000 ducats for our ransom; which sum was not paid, for that there were none, save only poor men'.[4] Sir William's self-professed Catholicism apparently caused him no scruples where money was concerned. By August, 1590, Sir William was still clinging tenaciously to his captives, and demanding as ransom the exhorbitant sum of 12,000 ducats.

By June, 1590, the number of prisoners in Sir William's care had mysteriously risen to 15. The Spanish prisoners had now become so desperate that they resorted to writing direct to the Queen, only to have their letter intercepted by Sir William, who, in the words of De Castillo, 'thrust us into a strong prison, giving us for our diet but bread, broth and water'.[5]

As for Pedro de Valdes, the most prestigious prisoner of them all, it was not until the spring of 1593 that he was released, by which time he had become something of a celebrity, and to celebrate the occasion, the Lord Mayor of London held a banquet in his honour. The ransom paid was £3550.

Drake would doubtless have been aware that Spanish prisoners were being held in Devonshire. But is it possible that former enemies of his from the *San Pedro Mayor* on their release, settled permanently in his native Devon, took up residence within a day's horse-ride of his home at Buckland Abbey, integrated into the local community, married and had children? If so, then such are the fortunes of war!

⁊

Meanwhile, as Drake's star was in the ascendant, so Sir Walter Raleigh's plummeted to the depths. A relief expedition sent in 1589 to Roanoke, found no trace of the colonists who had been set down there. In fact, none of them were ever seen again. Although Raleigh's aims may, in the context of the times, have seemed laudable and far-sighted, the loss sustained by him on his investment was in the order of £40,000.

16

Final Years, Drake's Last Voyage

Drake was henceforth to be found ashore at his mansion, Buckland Abbey, near Plymouth. In 1591, not content with the quiet life he and the Borough of Plymouth made a 'composytyon' (agreement) for the 'bringinge of the River of Meve (Meavy) to the towne', for which the town paid him the sum of £98.[1] The problem up until then was that the River Plym was being polluted by settlements upstream along its banks, forcing the citizens to travel over a mile in order to obtain a supply of water suitably safe to drink. The numerous ships berthed in the town's harbour faced the same predicament.

Work began in December, 1591, to build a stone-lined channel, or 'leat' from the River Meavy, high on the hills of Dartmoor, to a reservoir above the town. This was only 7 miles away as the crow flies, but the leat which wound its way through 'valleys, wastes and bogs, and what was most troublesome of all, a mighty rock, thought to be impenetrable', would be about 25 miles long on completion.[2]

The waterway was 'with great care and diligence effected', in the amazingly short time of four months, and on April 24, 1592, it was completed and came to be known as 'Drake's leat'. When the great day came, Drake, with the mayor and corporation, and 'amidst the firing of salutes' and in the presence of 'mounted trumpeters...

Sir Francis Drake, artist unknown.
Photo: National Portrait Gallery, London.

153

Drake's 'leat'.

rode beside the water as it flowed for the first time into the town'.[3]

As ever, there was an element of self-interest in the project. Drake, being the entrepreneur that he was, had a genius for helping others whilst benefiting himself at the same time. He had proved this on numerous occasions at sea. Now he was to prove it on land, as he set about building six 'greast milles (gristmills)': two at nearby Eggbuckland, and another four in Plymouth. These were in addition to the ones he already rented and operated at Millbay, on the north side of Plymouth Sound.

In 1592, Sir Walter Raleigh invested £34,000 in equipping a fleet which had great success when in the Azores, a Spanish carrack (large merchant ship, equipped for fighting), the *Madre de Dios* (bound for Spain from the East Indies), was captured with a cargo of jewels, spices, ivory, and silks to the value of £150,000. However, on his return, instead of receiving the wholesome praise of his Queen, Raleigh was sent to the Tower. This was because he had committed the cardinal sin of affecting undying love and devotion to his Sovereign (which all her courtiers did, if they were wise!) while, without her knowledge, paying court to the twenty-seven-year-old Elizabeth Throgmorton, one of her maids of honour – who was also sent to the Tower.

On their release two months later, the couple are believed to have married. Now banished from Court, they settled at Sherborne in Dorset, where Raleigh had obtained a lease on the castle and its adjoining parkland. Here he began to live dangerously, by associating with religious sceptics such as Thomas Harriot (a member of the 1585 expedition to Roanoke), Christopher Marlowe (dramatist and poet), and even his own brother, Carew. Matters came to a head when Thomas Howard, Viscount Bindon, was directed to examine Raleigh and his associates concerning their alleged heresies.

✺

In 1593, Drake once again represented Plymouth as its Member of Parliament. He strongly advocated carrying on the war with Spain, and busied himself with measures for strengthening the fortifications of the town, which in the previous century had twice been burned down (by roving French and Bretons). A fort was built to protect the entrance to the harbour, for which Drake contributed the sum of £100, and the fortifications of St Nicholas Island (where Drake was alleged to have taken shelter after the Catholic uprising of 1549 – subsequently known as 'Drake's Island') were improved and a guard established there.[1]

✺

Raleigh was fascinated by the story of the legend of the City of Manoa, in South America, known to the Spaniards as 'El Dorado'. Having first sent his servant out to explore the Orinoco (in what is now Venezuela), he himself sailed to Trinidad, where he captured and befriended its governor, Antonio de Berrio, who provided evidence to reinforce the legend. Raleigh himself now travelled to the Orinoco and sailed up it for a distance of about 450 miles, but failed to discover the fabled city. He returned to England with little more than some quartz, which contained some small grains of gold, and perhaps the earliest specimens of mahogany to be imported into the country.

✺

Late in 1594, Drake was commissioned by the Queen to take a new fleet to the Indies. He was to sail in his flagship the *Defiance*, with Hawkins in the *Garland* as vice admiral. This was a reversal of roles, for in their early days of slaving on the coast of Guinea, Hawkins had commanded, with Drake as his new apprentice. The total complement included 2500 soldiers under the command of Sir Thomas Baskerville.

The fleet of 26 ships and pinnaces (including six royal vessels provided by the Queen) did not leave Plymouth until September 7, 1595, by which time Drake's plans had been reported back to the King of Spain by amongst others, his old prisoner from the *Rosario*, Pedro de Valdes, who by now had been released. The Spaniards reacted by strengthening their navy and the defences of their ports, and carrying the war to England by raiding Cornwall and burning Penzance on its northern coast, together with other towns.

A landing at Gran Canaria on October 6 was initially repulsed by its Spanish defenders, and when a party went ashore the following day, some local shepherds set about Drake's men, killing some and capturing the rest. The surgeon of the ship *Solomon* was taken prisoner, and from him the Spaniards gained information as to the purpose of the expedition, and accordingly sent ships ahead to the Indies to warn of their approach.

Drake and Hawkins reached the Lesser Antilles (West Indies) on October 26, and Guadaloupe three days later. Two of the smaller English ships, the *Delight* and the *Francis*, fell behind, and in their efforts to catch up, sailed by mistake towards a Spanish fleet commanded by Don Pedro Tello de Guzman, which they mistook for their compatriots. The Spaniards gave chase, the *Francis* was captured and its crew taken prisoner, and the ship abandoned. As the *Delight* hurried to inform Drake of the news, so De Guzman, who guessed that the English were heading for Puerto Rico, hastened there himself.

Sir John Hawkins, Drake's kinsman and one time mentor, had not been well, and on November 21, with the ships at anchor off Puerto Rico, he died at the age of sixty-three.

That same evening, as Drake was eating supper with his officers, the ships suddenly came under fire from shore batteries. When shots penetrated *Defiance*, Drake's friend, Brutus Brown, was killed, and Sir Nicholas Clifford was wounded so badly that he died in the night. It is said that Drake's stool was shot from under him as he was in the act of drinking a cup of beer.

Having found a safer anchorage, Drake returned that night, entered the harbour and attacked the Spanish warships anchored there with fire bombs. However, the resulting fires illuminated the English ships for the gunners in the castle above, who succeeded in driving them away. Despite heavy loss of life, Drake remained optimistic, saying to Baskerville, 'I will bringe thee to twenty places foure (far) more wealthye and easier to bee gotten'.[5]

Before leaving, Drake sent a letter to the Governor of Puerto Rico, Pedro Xuarez, pointing out that during the action, his men had rescued some Spaniards after their ships were set on fire, and hoping in return that the 25 or more Englishmen, who had been taken prisoner by De Guzman when he captured their ship the *Francis*, would be similarly well treated.

A week later, the fleet was at Rio de la Hacha, on the Spanish Main, where the men were rested and the ships were refitted. Here there was little booty to be had; the inhabitants once again having been forewarned, apart from some pearls from the local pearl fishery. The citizens offered Drake a small ransom in pearls, but he, dissatisfied with the amount, departed on December 19, having ordered the town to be burnt. Having similarly looted and burnt settlements at Rancheria and Santa Marta, which they reached the following day, they sailed on to Nombre de Dios, arriving there on December 27. Again, the town was deserted and there was little to be found except for a bar of gold and a few pieces of silver. Two days later, Baskerville set out with about 900 men on the road to Panama, the idea being that when he had taken this town, Drake would sail up the Chagres River and join him with reinforcements.

At Capira Pass Baskerville's men found the slopes muddy and impass-able because of heavy rain, and were obstructed by Spanish troops who were lying in wait. Next morning, the Spaniards were reinforced and after a short battle, Baskerville was forced to retreat to Nombre de Dios.

On January 5, 1596, having set fire to Nombre de Dios, Drake sailed away westwards. He told army Captain Thomas Maynarde, 'God hath many things in store for us, and I knowe many meanes to do her maiestie (Her Majesty) good service, and to make us rich', but Maynarde noticed that Drake was depressed, and since their return from Panama, 'he never carried mirth nor ioy (joy) in his face'.[6]

At Escudo Island they destroyed two of their pinnaces, which were damaged, and constructed four more. By this time, an epidemic of fever ran through the fleet, with Drake himself suffering from bloody dysentery. On January 24, they set sail again but were thwarted by a lack of wind. Meanwhile, Drake's condition worsened and he took to his bed.

Before setting sail, Drake had made a will. This granted Buckland Abbey and its contents, together with the leases of the Plymouth grist mills, to Lady Elizabeth, his wife. To Thomas, his brother, he left properties in Plymouth, including the house in the High Street in which he now lived. Jonas Bodenham, his first wife's nephew, his lieutenant in many a sea-battle, and now captain of the *Adventure*, was left £100. Drake's servants received between 40 shillings and £100 each. The manors of Sampford Spiney, Sherford, and Yarcombe were not mentioned in the will, the reason being that under the terms of Drake's marriage contract, these were already guaranteed to Lady Drake for the period of her lifetime. To the poor of Plymouth he left the sum of £40.

Now at sea and about to die, Drake added a codicil to his will. Anxious that his property should 'remayne and continue in his own name and blood, to the good pleasure of Almighty God',[7] he named his brother Thomas, sole executor of his will, and his heir. Bodenham was to inherit Sampford Spiney, and Francis Drake of Esher (his godson and namesake), was to inherit Yarcombe on condition that he paid the sum of £2000 for it within two years.

Drake now summoned his officers to give them parting gifts, and to William Whitelocke, his servant, he gave plate and jewels. He then asked Whitelocke to clothe him in his armour, so that 'he might dy (die) like (a) soldier'.[8] Towards the end, he rose from his bed and 'made some speeches, but being brought to bed again, within one hour dyed' and 'yielded up his spirit like a Christian to his Creator, quietly in his cabin', on the morning of January 28, 1596.

With Baskerville now in command, Drake's body was sealed in a lead coffin which, to the sound of cannon and the lament of trumpets, was let down into the warm waters of Nombre de Dios Bay, a league out to sea off Porto Bello.

In their intention to sail on to Santa Marta and from there to Jamaica, the English were thwarted when they met a Spanish fleet off the Isla de Pinos, which scattered their ships. They had previously agreed that in such an eventuality, each would make its own way home to England. Drake's drum, together with his Bible and his sword, were brought back to Buckland Abbey and given to his widow. The unhappy event of Drake's death was faithfully recorded in Plymouth's Black Book. 'Sr Fraunces Drake and Sr John Hawkyns went to the West Indias with xxxvi sayles of shippes and pynnaces and both dyed in the Jurney and Sr Nicholas Clyfford slayne'.

Drake's Drum, Buckland Abbey.
Photo: National Trust.

With the death of Drake the fortunes of the English in the West Indies ebbed away. The Spaniards were now very much aware of the danger, and had taken steps to defend themselves accordingly. There were to be no more easy pickings.

&

These words, sufficient to stir the hearts of any true Englishman, were written by Sir Henry Newbolt three centuries later, in 1896:

> Take my drum to England, hang et by the shore,
>   Strike et when your powder's runnin' low;
> If the Dons sight Devon, I'll quit the port o' heaven,
>   An' drum them up the Channel as we drummed them long ago.

(Drake's drum was a side-drum or 'snare drum', 21 inches high, of a type used by foot regiments, with a shell or barrel of walnut. How he came by it is not known, but he took it with him on his final voyage in the *Defiance*.)

&

No finer epitaph to Drake can be imagined than that written by his nephew and namesake, Francis, son of Richard Drake of Esher: 'He was of stature low, but set and strong grown, a very religious man towards God and His houses, generally sparing churches wherever he came; chaste in his life, just in his dealings, true to his word; merciful to those that were under him, and hating nothing so much as idleness. In matters, especially those of moment, he was never wont to rely on other men's care, however trustworthy or skilful they might seem to be, but always contemning (despising) danger, and refusing no toil, he was wont himself to be one (the first), no matter who was a second, at every turn where courage, skill or industry was to be employed'.[9]

17

Finale

In April, 1590, Sir Francis Walsingham, who had never enjoyed good health, died in London at the age of sixty.

In 1591, a squadron of ships, six belonging to the Queen, with Sir Thomas Howard (cousin of the Lord Admiral) in command, was sent from Plymouth to the Azores to intercept the homeward bound treasure fleet of Spain. Sir Richard Grenville, from whom Drake had purchased Buckland Abbey, was vice admiral in command of the *Revenge*, Drake's former flagship from the Armada campaign. Although he had participated in the unsuccessful attempt to colonise Virginia, Sir Richard had little experience of naval warfare; this was to cost him his life.

Howard was lying off Flores (Azores) when the Spanish treasure fleet came into view. However, finding this fleet to be escorted by a powerful squadron of warships, Howard decided not to risk his ships against a clearly superior force, and therefore stood out to sea to avoid it. Grenville, on the other hand, instead of following Howard, took on the enemy single-handed. The result was predictable. Once in the lee of the high Spanish galleons, *Revenge* was becalmed and became easy prey. She was boarded, and after gallant resistance, overpowered. The mortally wounded Sir Richard was taken aboard the Spanish Admiral's ship *San Pablo*, where he died a few days later.

As for other ships which took part in the Armada campaign, Sir John Hawkin's *Victory* survived until 1608, and Captain George Raymond's *Elizabeth Bonaventure* was finally broken up in 1610, having been in service for over fifty years.

In 1596 a fleet, under the joint command of Howard and the Earl of Essex sailed for Spain to pre-empt another invasion attempt, in the course of which Sir Walter Raleigh, in command of the Warspite, made a successful raid on Cadiz, but was seriously wounded. At the end of the year, Lord Howard was created Earl of Nottingham.

Pedro de Valdes returned to Spain in the summer of 1594. In 1602 he was appointed Governor of Cuba. He retired in 1608 to his home town of Gijon on the north coast of Spain, and died in 1614.

In 1597, Elizabeth Drake married Sir William Courtenay. In 1598, after endless wrangling over Drake's will, a court upheld Lady Elizabeth's claim to have the codicil to Drake's will annulled, and to have the manors of Samford Spiney and Yarcombe returned to her. When her father died the same year, Elizabeth also inherited his estate of Combe Sydenham, and the manors of Sutton Bingham and Bossington. When Elizabeth herself died in that year, Sir Francis Drake's properties reverted to the Drake family, as had been his wish.

In 1599, the Spaniards made another invasion attempt, which was equally unsuccessful. Lord Charles Howard was now 'lord lieutenant general of all England', and sat on numerous commissions in 1603 to make preparations for the coronation of James I, and in 1604 to negotiate peace with Spain. He died in 1624, aged eighty-eight.

In 1601, Jonas Bodenham sold the manor of Sampford Spiney to Thomas Drake, who also recovered the manor of Yarcombe, when the Drakes of Esher failed to pay the price stipulated by Drake within the allotted time.

Raleigh had powerful enemies at Court, in particular the Queen's new favourite, Robert Devereux. James, son of Mary Queen of Scots, was aware that Raleigh was opposed to his claim to the English throne. Consequently, when after the death of Elizabeth on March 24, 1603, James crossed into England from Scotland, Raleigh was deprived of his position of captain of the guard, had his wine licences suspended, and was ordered out of his dwelling place, Durham House, on London's Strand.

On 17 July, 1603, Raleigh was again sent to the Tower. His misfortune was that he was a friend of the diplomat Henry Brooke, Lord Cobham, who in turn had corresponded with Count Aremberg, Spain's agent in London. At his trial in November in Winchester's Great Hall, he was found guilty of compassing (plotting) the death of the King (James I), and seeking to deliver his country into the hands of its enemy. Along with Cobham and Thomas, Baron Grey de Wilton, he was again committed to the Tower.

King Philip II of Spain died on September 12, 1598, at the age of seventy-one. Tumours had broken out all over his body, and he had spent the last few weeks of his life in such agony that he was unable to bear anything touching his skin. He was buried in a coffin made of timbers from a galleon which had fought against the English.

Philip had refused to regard the Armada expedition as a failure, preferring to blame his navy's defeat on the weather. His appetite for invading England was undimmed, and over the next fifteen years he dispatched, to this end, three more fleets, none of which was successful.

Queen Elizabeth outlived Philip by five years, dying in 1603, a lonely and miserable woman who still mourned the death of her favourite suitor, Robert Devereux, Earl of Essex, who was executed for treason in 1601. In the latter years of her reign, there was famine and food riots throughout the land, and a war with Ireland that was to last for nine years. Despite the triumph over the Armada, there would be no peace with Spain during her lifetime. She was buried in Westminster Abbey, which brought her nearer in death to Mary Queen of Scots (whose tomb was also to lie there), than ever she had been in life.

Elizabeth's death did not go unnoticed in Plymouth where, in the Black Book, it is recorded that she 'departed this mortall life at Richemonde the 24th daie of Marche (1603) in the morninge, and that same daie by nyne of the clocke, James the Kinge of Scotlande was p'claimed in London to be oure king of England... On the last day of that same month, his Ma'tie was proclaymed at the Markett Crosse here in Plymouth to be kinge of Englande... at which tyme here was greate trivmphe with Bondfiers, gunnes and ringinge of bells with other kinds of musicke'.

With the succession of James, the wheel of struggle between Protestantism and Catholicism might have turned full circle, had it not been for the fact that the new king had been brought up a Protestant.

In June, 1617, Raleigh, who had languished in the Tower for fourteen years, during which time he had written his *History of the World*, ventured all his and his wife's remaining wealth on another voyage to the Orinoco. Once more, the expedition was a failure, and twelve months later he arrived back in Plymouth. He was arrested shortly afterwards, and on October 29, 1618, beheaded in Old Palace Yard, which lay on the south side of Westminster Hall (site of the eleventh-century Palace of Edward the Confessor).

After the *Thomas Drake*, which fought in the Armada campaign, there would be another 23 sea-going ships bearing the name of 'Drake', over a period of more than three centuries. The last was an armoured, twin-screw cruiser of 14,100 tons, built at Pembroke Dock in South Wales and launched on March 5, 1901. She was capable of 24 knots. On October 2, 1917, she was torpedoed by a German U-Boat, U79 off Rathlin Island, off the north coast of Ireland. One officer and 18 men were killed in the explosion; the remainder of the crew were saved.

18

Epilogue

Drake's brilliance in seamanship, navigation, and naval tactics are unquestioned, but what was he really like as a person? Certainly, he was no lover of Roman Catholics, having as his role model his father, Edmund, an avid Protestant, who became a curate and vicar. Also, he lost two brothers, one in heroic circumstances at the hands of the Spaniards, and the other from disease sustained on an expedition against them. He also lost many of his men on such expeditions, including his beloved friend, John Oxenham. Drake would also have heard harrowing accounts told by the few Englishmen who returned home, having been taken prisoner by the Spaniards and who had been tortured and sent to be galley slaves. He had also witnessed at first hand the duplicity of the Spaniards at St Juan de Ulua; the memories of which remained with him for the rest of his days.

Miraculously, however, Drake retained his wit and sense of humour; and more importantly his sense of dignity by not allowing himself to sink to the level of barbarism practised by his opponents, despite being provoked to do so. He invariably treated his captives, whether Spanish or otherwise, with respect, and when setting them free was always careful to provide them with a ship and victuals. There were exceptions, but this must be seen in the context of the times. Numerous statements made by former prisoners of Drake affirm that he was no torturer or murderer, where people in his charge were concerned.

Nevertheless, Drake was strict when it came to matters of discipline. As his one-time prisoner, Francisco de Zarate said, 'He punishes the least fault'. However, according to Plymouth magistrate, Edmund Tremayne, as far as prize money was concerned, Drake 'would rather diminish his own portion, than leave any of them (his men) unsatisfied'. In fact, as far as his 'mariners and followers' were concerned, Tremayne himself had been an eye witness to 'such certain show of good will (by them towards Drake)', that he could not envisage that many of them would 'leave his company wheresoever (to go elsewhere)'.[1]

When his negro messenger boy was cut down in cold blood at Santa Domingo, Drake's anger for once got the better of him; in his determination to have the culprits brought to justice, he hanged two Spanish friars whom he was keeping as prisoners. On another occasion when he suspected the captive Jacome from the bark *Diaz Bravo* of concealing gold pesos aboard his ship, Jacome refused to talk, Drake had him suspended over and dropped into the sea (quickly to be rescued), with the intention not of inflicting gratuitous violence, but as a last ditch attempt to get information. Although Drake's action was harsh, Jacome seems to have suffered no lasting harm as a result. For Drake, the acquisition of booty and treasure was a serious business. He also reverted to drastic action on his circumnavigation, when he had Thomas Doughty tried and executed, having previously given one whom he had considered a friend, the benefit of the doubt. This was because he realised that without such action the whole expedition would be jeopardised by Doughty, who was trying to undermine it.

Drake could appear to be impulsive at times: as at Cadiz, when he was criticised by William Borough; and in his pursuit of the *Rosario*, when he was criticised by Martin Frobisher. At other times he planned meticulously, as for example when he sought out the safe anchorage at Port Pheasant; and when he raided the mule train near Nombre de Dios. Nevertheless, he almost invariably achieved his objectives.

His attention to detail was no small factor in his success, and he was always careful to careen his ship and take on an adequate supplies of fresh water and victuals.

Drake showed immense qualities of leadership, particularly during the vicious and prolonged storms which assailed him for more than fifty consecutive days off Cape Horn during the circumnavigation, and again when the *Golden Hind* ran aground on a reef off Indonesia. His men loved him, regarded him as a talisman, and when he was wounded at Nombre de Dios, begged him to return to his ship, (which he refused to do until their mission was completed), their fear being for his safety.

Edmond Howes, who continued the seventeenth-century English chronicler John Stow's 'Chronicles' after Stow's death, describes Drake as being '... more skilful in all poyntes of Navigation, than any that ever was before his time, in his time, or since his death...'. Drake was also '... of a perfect memory, great Observation, Eloquent by Nature, Skilful in Artillery...' and '... Expert and apt to let blood (for medicinal purposes, of course!), and give Physicke unto his people according to the Climats'. However, there was a caveat, for in Howes' eyes, Drake had three 'imperfections', in that he was 'Ambitious for Honor', 'Unconstant in Amity (making friendly relationships)', and 'Greatly affected to Popularity'.[2]

Drake showed no bitterness at being appointed vice admiral in the Armada campaign, instead of admiral; even Lord Howard admitted that Drake was far more experienced than he was for the job. 'I must not omit to let you know.' Howard told Walsingham, 'how lovingly and kindly Sir Francis Drake beareth himself; and how dutifully to Her Majesty's service and unto me...'

But perhaps Drake's greatest regret was that he was never made a member of the Queen's Privy Council, despite his great and proven abilities. Against him was the fact that he had come from nothing, so in the eyes of the Council he was an upstart, an outsider. Equally galling for Drake was the attitude of the 'Nobles and Chiefest' of the Court (i.e. Lord Burghley and the Earl of Sussex), who refused 'that Gold and Silver which he presented them with, as if he had not legally come by it'.[3]

Even though in his battles against the Armada, Drake was fighting for his Queen, in his heart he was more of a pirate; as demonstrated when he temporarily abandoned his post to pursue the *Rosario*. Martin Frobisher's assertion however, that he was a coward, is simply not borne out by events.

When not at sea he made strenuous efforts as Member of Parliament for Plymouth, to have money made available to improve the town's water supply, and strove equally hard to improve its defensive fortifications.

Drake treated women with respect and consideration, and expected others to do the same, as shown during the raid on Panama. He had no children by either of the two women he had married, and this may have been a source of regret to him. Nevertheless, he had a godson, his namesake Francis, son of his kinsman, Francis Drake of Esher in Surrey. Drake made it clear that the boy could expect no legacy on his death; though he did present him with a jewel and a purse of money. The bulk of Drake's fortune would go to his younger brother Thomas, who married in 1587, the year prior to the Armada's defeat. Thomas also had a son named Francis.

Drake showed his humanity on numerous occasions, and it is difficult to disagree with Wagner's assertion that he was 'neither cruel nor blood-thirsty, but on the contrary, had a kindly disposition and a great sense of humour'. He released Cimaroon slaves (even though it must be admitted that he himself had once participated in the transportation of slaves). He refused to exact vengeance on the natives of the islands of Mocha (when his men were assailed with arrows and two of them were hacked to death before his eyes), when he could easily have done so, because he realised that they had mistaken the English for the cruel and hated Spaniards. He treated San Juan de Anton, captain of the *Nuestra de la Concepcion*, and Don Pedro de Valdez, admiral of the Andalucian squadron and commander of the *Nuestra Senora del Rosario* with the utmost chivalry, enjoyed their company, dined with them, and exchanged gifts and ideas.

An irony of his life is that he, a staunch Protestant, chose for a home, the former Cistercian monastery of Buckland. Equally ironic is that after his death, his widow Lady Elizabeth married the infamous Catholic, Sir William Courtenay, whose callousness in the treatment of the Spanish prisoners in his care contrasted so strongly with that of Drake.

Note on Chapters

CHAPTER 1.
1. Jenkins, F.P.
2. Nichols, P. *Sir Francis Drake Revived*, Preface.
3. Wagner, H.R., p.317.
4. Canterbury Cathedral Archives.
5. *Sir Francis Drake Revived*, Preface.

CHAPTER 2.
1. Camden, W., *Annales Rerum Anglicarum*, (i), Book 2, pp.417-8.
2. Hakluyt, R., *William Hawkins's Voyages*, pp.20-21.
3. Hakluyt, R., *The First Voyage of John Hawkins*, pp.98-99.
4. *Dictionary of National Biography (DNB)*, Hawkins, pp.213.
5. Hakluyt, R., *The Third Voyage of John Hawkins*, pp.103-114.

CHAPTER 3
1. Wagner, H.R., pp.317.
2. *Sir Francis Drake Revived*, pp.54-104.
3. Hakluyt, R., *The Travels of Job Hortrop*, pp.114-136.
4. Wagner, H.R., pp.305.

CHAPTER 4.
1. Clarke, S., *Marrow of Ecclesiastical History*, pt.ii, Life of Queen Elizabeth, ed. 1675.
2. Public Record Office (PRO) PC2/6, pp.487-8.
3. Klarwill, V. 193; Pollen, Mary's letter to the Duke of Guise, 41.
4. Neale, J.E., *Elizabeth I and Her Parliaments*, 1559-81 (London 1953) i. p.49.
5. Speech to Parliament, 1586. Camden, W., Annales, p.98.
6. Neale, J.E., *Elizabeth I and Her Parliaments*, 1559-81 (London 1953), p.192; State Papers (SP)12/71/16.

CHAPTER 5.
1. Principal reference for this chapter, Francis Drake (junior), *The World Encompassed*, pp.127-205, and Wagner, H.R.
2. Mendoza to Philip II, 9 January 1581, Hume, M.A., 3:73-5.
3. 'More Light on Drake', *Mariners' Mirror*, April 1930.
4. http://website.lineone.net/-peter.bond/page3.htm.
5. Nuttall, Z., op.cit. pp.302-3.
6. Wagner, H.R., p.339.
7. Wagner, H.R., p.300.
8. John Cooke in *The World Encompassed*, p.213.
9. Diary of Richard Madox, 12 September 1582, in Donno, E.S., *An Elizabethan in 1582*, p.184.

10. John Cooke in *The World Encompassed*, p.213.
11. Wagner, H.R., p.36.

CHAPTER 6.
1. Wagner, H.R., p.119.
2. Wagner, H.R., p.365.
3. Wagner, H.R., p.374.
4. Wagner, H.R., p.374.
5. Wagner, H.R., p.376.
6. Wagner, H.R., p.376.
7. British Library (BL), Harley Manuscript 280, fol. 86v.
8. Francisco Gomez, Rengifo (Nuttall, pp.352-3).
9. Wagner, H.R., p.311.

CHAPTER 7.
1. John Drake, First Declaration (Nuttall, p.32).
2. *The World Encompassed*, Additional Notes, pp.217-218.
3. Wagner, H.R., *Anonymous Narrative*, p.282.
4. Dispatch to Sir Francis Walsingham, 17 May, 1587. *Navy Records Society*, vol xi (1898), p.134.
5. Testimony of Lawrence Eliot, et al, of the *Golden Hind*, SP Dom. 12/144, No 17ii, see British Library Exhibition Catalogue, *Sir Francis Drake*, items 101-2.

CHAPTER 8.
1. John Drake, Second Declaration (Nuttall, p.54).
2. Camden, W., Annales ii, 360.
3. Wagner, H.R., p.306.
4. Wagner, H.R., p.322.
5. PRO, Warrants for the Great Seal Series II (c.82) bundle 1380.
6. Plymouth, Black Book, p.19.
7. *DNB*, Raleigh p.632.
8. Monson, Sir W., 'Naval Tracts' in Churchill, *Voyages* iii, p.147.
9. Hakluyt, R., *The Second Voyage of Martin Frobisher*, p.156.
10. The Leicester Journal, BL Harley Ms 2202 fols 57v-58.
11. Keeler, M.F., *Drake's West Indian Voyage*, 5.
12. S.P. Flanders, 1587, No.32, July 28 (draft).

CHAPTER 9
1. Pollen, J.H., *Babington Plot*, pp.21-22.
2. Camden, W., *Annals* (1688), Book 3, p.202.
3. Hakluyt, R., *Drake and the Spanish Fleet*, pp.352-357.
4. Drake to Burghley, 2 April 1587, PRO SP Dom. Elizabeth 200/2.
5. Walsingham to Sir Edward Stafford, 21 April 1587 in Hopper, C., p.29.
6. Council to Drake, undated, PRO SP Dom. Elizabeth 200/17.
7. Hakluyt, R., pp.352-357.

8. British Library (BL) Harley MS 7002, fol. 8.
9. Bacon, F., *Considerations touching the war with Spain* (Harleian Misc. 1745, vol.v, p85, col.1).
10. *SP Dom*. 200/4b; Corbett, J.S., *Spanish War*, pp.107-109.
11. Burghley to De Loo, 28 July 1587, Butler, A.J., State Papers, Foreign, vol 21, part 3, p.186.
12. B.L. Lansdowne, MS 52 No 39, fol.108.
13. 30 March 1588, Barrow, J., p.275.

CHAPTER 10.
Principal reference for Chapters 10-14, Motley, J.L.
1. Maura Gamazo, Gabriel, p.121.
2. *Calendar of State Papers (CSP) Spanish*, May 1588.
3. Wright, T., *Queen Elizabeth*, ii. 385.
4. PRO SP 12/209/40 fol.58.
5. Ibid.
6. *DNB*, Elizabeth, p.640.
7. As 6. above.
8. as 6. above.
9. PRO SP 12/209/40 fol.58v.
10. Laughton, J.K., *Armada Papers*, Vol.I, p.256.
11. Drake to the Queen, 13 April 1588, PRO SP 12/209/89, fol.134v.
12. Laughton, J.K., *Armada Papers*, Vol.II, p.331.
13. Ibid, Vol.I, p.256.

CHAPTER 12.
1. Corbett, J.S., *Drake and the Tudor Navy* 2:177.
2. *SP Dom*. 12/212 No.135.
3. Hakluyt, R., p.376.
4. Deposition of Matthew Starke, 11 August 1588, PRO SP Domestic 12/214/63-64, fols.139-40v, pp.141-2.
5. Pine, J., *The Tapestry Hangings in the House of Lords; representing several engagements between the English and Spanish fleets in... 1588...*, (2nd edn. 1753).
6. Hakluyt, R., *The Spanish Armada*, p.377.
7. Laughton, J.K., *Armada Papers*, Vol.I, p.9.
8. PRO SP 12/215/49 (Laughton, Vol.II, pp.152-153).

CHAPTER 13.
1. Drake to Walsingham, August 20, 1588 in Barrow, 310.
2. Wynter to Walsingham, August 11, 1588 (S.P. Office MS).
3. Howard to Walsingham, August 8, 1588 (S.P. Office MS).
4. Drake to Walsingham, in Barrow, 301.
5. Herrera, A. de, III. iii, 110.
6. *Cal. State Papers Dom.*, 29 July.

CHAPTER 14.
1. Drake to Walsingham, August 10, 1588 in Barrow, 304.
2. Howard to Walsingham, August 17, 1588 in Barrow, 306, 307.
3. Drake to the Queen, August 8, 1588, Cal. State Papers, Dom.
4 Howard to Walsingham, August 17, 1588 in Barrow, 306.
5. Howard to Walsingham, August 18, 1588 (S.P. Office MS).
6. Philip II to Parma, October 10, 1588 (Arch. de Simancas, MS).
7. Philip II to Parma, October 10, 1588 (Arch. de Simancas, MS).
8. Drake in Stone, 750 seq.
9. Howard to Burghley, August 20, 1588 (S.P. Office MS).
10. Seymour to Walsingham, September 2, 1588 (S.P. Office MS).
11. Matthew Starke, August 20, 1588 (S.P. Office MS).
12. Drake to Walsingham, August 18, 1588 (S.P. Office MS).
13. Froude, J., xii. pp.433-4.
14. Elizabeth I, *Collected Works* (Chicago 2000), pp.325-6.
15. Justin de Nassau to Walsingham, August 27, 1588 (S.P. Office MS).
16. Philip II to Parma, September 3, 1588 (Arch. de Simancas).
17. Philip II to Parma, September 15, 1588 (Arch. de Simancas).
18. PRO SP 12/218/4 (Laughton II, p.290).
19. Acts of the Privy Council of England (APCE) xvi 328-9.

CHAPTER 15.
1. Queen to Norris and Drake, 7 July 1589, PRO SP Dom. Elizabeth 225/15.
2. PRO Sp 12/218/4 (Laughton II, pp.290-1).
3. APCE, xvi, 373-4.
4. Martin, P., p.57.
5. Martin, P., p.57.

CHAPTER 16
1. Plymouth, Black Book, p.20.
2. *Devon Worthies* by W.J.H. Phipps, pp.44-5.
3. Eliott-Drake, Lady E., p.111.
4. Eliott-Drake, Lady E., p.109.
5. Maynarde, T., *Sir Francis Drake and His Voyage*, 1595, BL Add. MS 5,209, fol.13v.
6. Ibid, fol.26v.
7. Eliott-Drake, Lady E., p.125.
8. Hakluyt, R., *The voyage truely discoursed*, Third and Last Volume, p.588.
9. *Devon Worthies*, p.46.

CHAPTER 18. (EPILOGUE)
1. *State Papers, Domestic, Elizabeth*, Vol.144, No.17.
2. Wagner, H.R., p.307.
3. Camden, W., *Annales* (1635), p.426.

Appendix 1

Notes on Sources

1. Richard Hakluyt, *Voyages and Documents*, selected by Janet Hampden.

Born in 1552, Richard Hakluyt was an M.A. of Christ Church, Oxford, and a clergyman by profession. However, reading about voyages of exploration and discovery was his principal interest; collecting and transcribing the accounts. His sources were the various seafarers whom he befriended, including Francis Drake, and also material which he obtained from the Bodleian Library in Oxford, where he studied and gave lectures in the 1570s. In some of his collected documents the name of the author is recorded; in others, unfortunately, it is not.

Although few of the original manuscripts which Hakluyt drew upon have seen the light of day for many centuries, those that are in existence bear witness to the fact that his transcriptions of them are faithful, and can therefore be trusted by scholars. In 1602, he became canon of Westminster Abbey. He died in 1616.

These accounts include 'William Hawkins' Voyages to Guinea and Brazil'(1530 and 1532); 'John Hawkins' 1st, 2nd and 3rd Voyages to the West Indies' (1562-3, 1564, and 1567-8) the 3rd of which was written by Hawkins himself; 'Francis Drake's Raid on Panama' (1572-3), a brief account by Lopez Vaz, a Portuguese; 'Francis Drake's circumnavigation' (1577-80) – anonymous; 'Francis Drake's attack on Cadiz' (1587) – anonymous; and the 'Invincible Armada' (1588) – by Emmanuel van Meteran, a Dutch historian resident in London.

2. *Sir Francis Drake Revived*, and *The World Encompassed* by Sir Francis Drake were issued jointly by Philip Nichols and Sir Francis Drake's nephew and namesake, Francis Drake junior.

Sir Francis Drake Revived (1626, by Christopher Ceely, Ellis Hickson and Philip Nichols, preacher), gives a far more detailed account of Drake's raid on Panama than appears in Hakluyt.

The World Encompassed by Sir Francis Drake (1628), which was written by Francis Drake junior, draws extensively on notes made by Francis Fletcher, chaplain, and on various anonymous narratives; one of which is included in Hakluyt, and on the narrative of the voyage by John Cooke, who sailed in the *Elizabeth* under Captain Winter and therefore only travelled as far as the Straits of Magellan.

Arriving at an objective assessment of the character of Sir Francis Drake is problematical in that, of the contemporary sixteenth century accounts, The Raid on Panama (*Sir Francis Drake Revived*) was revised and enlarged upon by Drake himself, and the account of his circumnavigation (*The World Encompassed*) was written by his nephew. Also many of Drake's letters still survive, which may not provide an altogether unbiased account.

However, for the Third Voyage of John Hawkins to the West Indies (Hakluyt) in which Drake participated, we have Hawkins' own account; for the Spanish Armada episode we have the account of Emmanuel van Meteran (also Hakluyt); for Drake's attack on Cadiz we have the Anonymous Account (also Hakluyt); and for Drake's voyage of circumnavigation as far as the Straits of Magellan, we have the account of John Cooke, sailor in the ship Elizabeth (who is far from flattering to Drake!).

Appendix 2

Literal Translation of the Names of the Spanish Ships

Barca de Amburg	Barque of Hamburg
Barca de Danzig	Barque of Danzig
Castillo Negro	Black Castle
El Gran Grifon	The Great Griffin
El Gran Grin	The Great Boar
Falcon Blanco Mediano	Little White Falcon
Galeon de Florencia	Galleon of Florence
Girona	Girona
La Conception de Juan de Cano	The Vision of John of Cano
La Lavia	The Lavia
La Maria Juan	The Mary John
La Rata Encoronda	The Crowned Rat
Le Regazona	The Mother's Lap
La Trindad Valencera	The Brave Trinidad
Nuestra Senora de Begona	Our Lady of Begona

Nuestra Senora de Pilar *De Zaragoza*	Our Lady of the Pillar of Zaragosa
Nuestra Senora del Rosario	Our Lady of the Rosary
Nuestra Senora del Socorro	Our Lady of Succour
San Cristobal	St Christopher
San Esteban	St Stephen
San Juan Bautista	St John the Baptist
San Juan de Portugal	St John of Portugal
San Felipe	St Philip
San Lorenzo	St Lawrence
San Luis	St Louis
San Martin	St Martin
San Mateo	St Matthew
San Pedro	St Peter
San Pedro Mayor	St Peter the Great
San Salvador	St Salvador (Saviour)
Santa Ana	St Anne
Santa Maria de la Rosa	St Mary of the Rose
Santiago	St James
Zuniga	Zuniga

Appendix 3

Definitions

A 'privateer' holds a commission from a government to attack only the ships of nations designated by that government. However, as a 'pirate' is self employed as it were, any ship is 'fair game'.

The 'Julian' calendar was instituted by Julius Caesar in 46 BC. In 1582 it was adjusted by Pope Gregory XIII to eliminate the error caused by the faulty calculation of the length of one year. At the time of the Armada most of Europe, including Spain, was using the 'Gregorian' Calendar. England, however, together with her colonies, continued to use the 'Old Style' Julian Calendar until 1752, when the error amounted to eleven days. Dates here are given in 'New Style' (i.e. Gregorian).

Of the following, there were roughly four to the English £1: ducats, escudos, scudi, crowns, pistolets, and gold coins.

Bibliography

Barrow, John. *The Life, Voyages, and Exploits of Admiral Sir Francis Drake*. London, 1843.

Brimacombe, Peter. *All the Queen's Men*. Sutton Publishing, 2000.

Bundeville, Thomas. *Description of Universal Mappes and Cardes*. London, 1589.

Calendar of Letters and State Papers relating to English Affairs, Archives of Simancas. Edited by Martin A. S. Hume. London, 1892-1899, 4 vols.

Calendar of State Papers, Colonial Series, 1862-92, 8 vols.

Camden, William. *Annales Rerum Anglicarum, et Hibernicarum. London 1615. Annales, The True and Royall History of the famous Empress Elizabeth*. London, 1625. (Translated by A. Darcie.)

Clamp, Arthur L. *Hope Cove and its People Remembered*, and *Sir Francis Drake and the Spanish Armada*.

Colin Martin and Gefferey Parker. *The Spanish Armada*. Guild Publishing, 1988.

Corbett, Sir Julian's. *Sir Francis Drake*. London and New York, 1890, and *Drake and the Tudor Navy*. London, 1898. New Edition, 1899.

Dictionary of National Biography. Smith, Elder & Co., London, 1885.

Ditmas, E.M.R. *The Legend of Drake's Drum*. West Country Folklore No. 6, 1973.

Eliott-Drake, Lady. *The Family and Heirs of Sir Francis Drake*. Smith, Elder & Co., London, 1911.

Fernandez-Armesto, Felipe. *The Spanish Armada*. Oxford University Press, 1988.

Hakluyt, Richard. *Voyages and Documents*, selected by Janet Hampden. Oxford University Press, Oxford, 1958.

Hampden, John. *Francis Drake, Privateer – contemporary narratives and documents, selected and edited by John Hampden*. Eyre Methuen, London, 1972.

Hawkins, John. *A True Declaration of the Troublesome Voyage of Mr John Hawkins... 1567 and 1568*. London, 1569.

Jenkins, Frances P. *The Benedictine Abbey of St. Mary and St. Rumon*. Tavistock Parochial Church Council, 1999.

Kelsey, Harry. *Sir Francis Drake, – the Queen's Pirate*. A Yale Nota Bene book. Yale University Press, 1998.

Keppel-Jones, P.T., and Wans, J. *Drake of Crowndale*. Devon County Council Local History Library.

Laughton, Sir John. *Armada Papers, Vol II - ed. state papers relating to the defeat of the Spanish Armada, Anno 1588*. Navy Records Society, 1894.

Loades, David. *The Chroniclers of the Tudor Queens*. Sutton Publishing Ltd, Stroud, Gloucestershire, 2002.

Martin, Paula. *Spanish Armada Prisoners*. Exeter Maritime Studies No. 1, 1988.

Milton, Giles. *Big Chief Elizabeth*. Hodder and Stoughton, London, 2000.

Motley, John Lowthrop. *History of the United Netherlands*. John Murray, London, 1875.

Nichols, Philip. *Sir Francis Drake Revived*. (Reviewed also by Sir Francis Drake himself before his death.) London, 1626.

Nuttall, Zelia. *New Light on Drake*. Hakluyt Society. London, 1914.

Phipps, W.J.H. *Devon Worthies*.

Stow, John. *The Chronicles of England, from Brute unto this present yeare of Christ, 1580*. London.

Treasures of the Armada. Exhibition at Plymouth City Museum and Art Gallery, 1-28 July, 1988.

Wagner, Henry R. *Sir Francis Drake's Voyage around the World*. John Howell. San Francisco, California, 1926.

World (the) Encompassed. By Sir Francis Drake, 'carefully collected out of the notes of Master Francis Fletcher, Preacher in this imployment and diuers others his followers in the same'. London, 1628.